Spiritualism And Charlatanism Or, The Tricks Of The Media

Pendie L. Jewett

Publishing Statement:

This important reprint was made from an old and scarce book.

Therefore, it may have defects such as missing pages, erroneous pagination, blurred pages, missing text, poor pictures, markings, marginalia and other issues beyond our control.

Because this is such an important and rare work, we believe it is best to reproduce this book regardless of its original condition.

Thank you for your understanding and enjoy this unique book!

NOTICE.

A PORTION of the *exposé* of the "Committee" was originally published in the New-York *World* of Sunday, March
16th, 1873, and is here reproduced by permission, having
been revised and extended by the author.

The primary object of this publication is to expose the
tricks and chicanery of a large and growing class of men
and women, who, trading upon the most tender and sacred
emotions of our nature, obtain money from the public on
pretense of giving communications from departed friends.

NEW-YORK, March, 1873.

SPIRITUALISM.

CHAPTER I.

It was early in February. The clock had struck four, and the busy hum of Wall street was beginning to sink to rest. Not a very eventful day. Cotton had been quiet and easier both for "spot" and "future." The London quotations came about steady for consols, and strong and higher for the '67's and new fives. The money market more active, with an advance in the rate on call to the exceptional extreme of 1-16 per cent. The gold market opened weak, and fell off to 112¼, but the gold clique, in a fresh turn of the windlass, raised the price to 113⅝. Railroad bonds buoyant, Southern securities steady, and Governments strong. Stocks heavy and lower. There had been more animation in some departments of trade, but, as a general thing, the markets were quiet and unchanged. A defalcation in a government office had kept the reporter of a morning paper very busy during the day, hunting up the details.

Coupés began to collect on the street, and well-dressed gentlemen to stand on the corner and hail the omnibuses as they passed. Business life became absorbed in the social and domestic as the current surged up-town.

In an office on Broadway, just out of Wall street, were collected a party of seven gentlemen, all of whom had been more or less interested in the various operations which I have sketched, and which formed the subject of a desultory conversation for a few moments. Their minds were evidently jaded by them, however, and their attention was readily turned to a slim-built, angular young man, who had been the last to enter, when he began to recount certain alleged wonderful manifestations by a spirit-medium, which had been told to him by a friend, and which he pronounced "humbug," with perhaps more energy than the occasion required.

"I tell you, gentlemen," he said, "these media are the greatest frauds of the age, not even excepting the operators in Wall street."

"Don't be personal or violent," said a gold broker. "Have you a cigar about you?"

"I attended a lecture at Apollo Hall recently," said a solemn-looking merchant, "when the speaker was a trance-medium. I went to sleep during the discourse, but, as far as I understood her, she attempted to explain every thing on the basis of 'the ineffable.'"

"Pooh!" said a banker of waggish tendencies, "'the scintillations of propinquity' beat that hollow."

"It is harder to spell," said a broker.

"Gentlemen," continued the angular young man, "your minds evidently need relaxation. That is well. Relax them; but don't jest on serious things concerning which you know little. Spiritualism is a natural phase of the human mind. It is a necessity. It has grown up out of man's nature and his teachings ; but the mass of its reputed high-priests are swindlers. I am preparing an article on the subject. I will read you the introduction."

"Heaven help us !" said a banker.

"Is it long?" asked a broker.

"Stand up !" exclaimed a merchant.

"Gentlemen, I ask you to listen in the interest of science."

"Tyndall's lectures always bored me," said an elegantly-dressed young man, who had not before spoken.

"Gentlemen!" (reading): "Until a comparatively recent date in the history of the human race, all the mysteries of nature were explained on the theory of supernatural agency. In the first efforts of his mind to grasp at the cause of phenomena, man endowed every object which his senses contemplated with life ; and the stars moved, the vegetation sprang up and increased, the rivers flowed on toward the sea, by their own volition. As in process of time his mind gradually developed out of this primitive idea, he adopted the theory of guardian spirits, or tutelar deities, by whose instrumentality all the operations of nature, which he saw around him, were carried on. Then it was the gentle fairy made her luxuriant home within the petals of the lily, and, with her companions, danced upon the greensward, within frequent sight of the awe-struck, belated peasant ; the elves peopled the air, and, reposing on the leaves of the trees, were rocked to sleep by the breezes ; gentle naiads of that beauty which makes nudity chaste——"

"Which ?" says a broker.

"—made music in the gurgling of every stream, and the sprites and fairies haunted every dell. The dwarfs and trolls indulged in mad revels within the hills and mounds, and genii led the way of fortunate mortals to caverns of enchantment and untold treasure."

"How would such an operation affect the market in these days ?" asked a broker.

"Let us be calm and non-resistant," responded the banker ; "he may die."

"Gradually as the mind of man still farther expanded, and he began to have a knowledge and appreciation of general laws as affecting phenomena, his deities grew less and less, being absorbed in a smaller number with more extended powers, until, in the end, they all centred in one omnipotent Creator and Preserver, in whose will and power lay a solution of all mystery. While retaining this idea of a supreme originator of all things, as a necessary base upon which his mind may rest, as one after the other of the various phenomena of nature has, by patient study and investigation, been explained, man has constantly tended toward the conclusion that they are all the result of certain immutable laws, and, in proportion to his approach thereto, have his fetishes, his tutelar deities and guardian spirits been driven to the wall, until in his more advanced stage, as represented by men of science, he has discarded them altogether. And yet, such is the influence of past teaching, increasing and intensifying as it moves along down the line of hereditary descent, that the mass of mankind, in the present day, retain, in some form, a belief in direct supernatural agency, affecting the matters of this life, and instinctively turn thereto for an explanation of any thing beyond their experience or ken."

"Hold there!" exclaimed the merchant. "Let us be orthodox or nothing. I yield you up the media, but make no attacks on the faith of our fathers."

"Your fathers believed according to their light. I am endeavoring to increase yours. Restrain yourself. I am coming to that."

"Is it long?" asked the broker.

"There are few who doubt that we are entering upon a new era of thought, in which the theological and metaphysical teachings of the past, to which primarily this belief in the active interference of spirits with the affairs of this life is due, are to be submitted to the severest test. If they stand this test, they will come out purified as by fire. If, on the contrary, they are consumed in the crucible, no harm can result which time can not rectify; for truth is in accordance with the natural laws which affect man, as well as all else, and only error can be destroyed. An investigation based upon the cumulative knowledge and experience of the past, and a continued study of all phenomena, in the light of that revelation resulting from the discoveries of science, is the controlling idea of this era. And in this investigation, no assumption of spirits is allowed. There is no longer admitted to be a *personal* responsibility in matters unexplained. Man is in the infancy of his knowledge. Even the functions of certain organs in his body are, as yet, imperfectly understood. That there are latent, undeveloped powers within his organism, destined to place him upon a much higher plane in the scale of existence, possibly to advance him to that point which he has been wont to regard - as the supernatural, is being dimly perceived. This advancement, whether it come sooner or later, will be in and of himself and without extraneous assistance. That in the phenomena of Mesmerism, Psychology, Psychometry, and so-called modern Spiritualism may be seen the first faint gleams of light which precede the glorious morning, is possible, and if so, man, unaided by the beings of another world, must deal with them alone, and alone reap the reward of his labors."

" Wait !" said the banker, " you are admitting too much. Once concede there are phenomena which can be explained on the basis of no known law, and the Spiritualists ask nothing farther. They regard their case as made out."

"And what then ?" responded the angular young man. "Do you take me for a pettifogging lawyer? Can you destroy a truth by denying it ? Is it any the less a truth because the weak and foolish distort it ?"

"I don't know about these phenomena," said the banker's

partner, who had been quietly listening ; "if they exist, I prefer to find some rational explanation of them, of course. But I object to spiritualism on quite another ground. It seems clear to me that, if we have an existence hereafter, it is as complete in its inception and continuance, as in accordance with some immutable law which prescribes its character and conditions and defines its duties, which perhaps gives to it pleasures and pains, as in the present. We see that man has high duties to perform in this world, which he can not avoid without the severest penalties. Isn't it rational to conclude that in another and higher sphere of existence and conscious entity, if such there be, man will have his duties correspondingly high and more difficult of avoidance ; that in another world he will meet others like him, and in his relations to them and the pursuits evolved therefrom, his existence will be passed? Reasoning from all analogy, the harmony, the completeness of nature forbid that a being can be an inhabitant of two worlds, holding a divided allegiance and incompatible relations. Certainly those who have passed the dark river and entered upon another and more advanced existence, have not done so to lead a life of vagabondage, nor do they remain here at the beck of those of whom to say little is to be charitable.

> 'Imperious Cæsar, dead and turned to clay,
> Might stop a hole to keep the wind away.'

But I doubt if George Washington and a great number of other worthies have gone into the show-business and are engaged in tipping tables and answering foolish questions in a still more foolish manner, through ignorant charlatans, few of whom know how to spell."

"Bravo !" exclaimed the merchant, " I also doubt. But what evidence of these phenomena is there ?"

"Plenty," responded the angular young man. "Of

course, I leave out the evidence of the spiritualists themselves, with whom 'the wish is father to the thought,' most of whom are incapable of distinguishing between impression and fact, and are, as a class, the most easily deluded people under the sun. Perhaps as satisfactory proof as any that has been furnished, is contained in a report of a committee appointed by the London Dialectical Society, in February, 1869, to examine and report upon the pretensions of Spiritualism. It may be found in a work entitled *Spiritualism answered by Science*. By Edward W. Cox, S.L., F.R.G.S., and made after a careful and exhaustive investigation of these phenomena, extending during a year, and in a manner and under conditions which absolutely preclude all idea of deception. I have embodied the gist of it in my article. Listen :

" 'The result of their (the committee's) long-continued and carefully conducted experiments, after trial by every detective test they could devise, has been to establish conclusively :

" ' First. That under certain bodily or mental conditions of one or more of the persons present, a force is exhibited sufficient to set in motion heavy substances without the employment of any muscular force, without contact or material connection of any kind between such substances and the body of any person present.

" 'Second. That this force can cause sounds to proceed, distinctly audible to all present, from solid substances not in contact with nor having visible or material connection with the body of any person present, and which sounds are proved to proceed from such substances by the vibrations which are distinctly felt when they are touched.

" 'Third. That this force is frequently directed by intelligence.'

" Without for a moment attributing the force or the exercise of this intelligence to the agency of spirits, the committee conclude their report as follows :

" ' Your committee express their unanimous opinion that the one important physical fact thus proved to exist, that *motion may be produced in solid bodies without material contact, by some hitherto unrecognized force, operating within an undefined distance from the human organism and beyond range of muscular action*, should be subjected to further scientific examination, with a view to ascertain its source, nature, and power.'

"This committee comprised men of various pursuits and capacities—ingenious lawyers, practiced scientists, skillful doctors, authors, artists, and shrewd men of business. The meetings were held at the private residences of members, and no professional medium was employed. It would seem therefore absurd to question their conclusions as to the facts."

"Did the committee furnish no theory in regard to these manifestations?" asked the merchant.

"None," was the response. "The author of the work to which I have referred, a prominent member of the committee, argues that it is the result of nerve or, as he styles it, psychic force, which proceeds from or, in some unknown manner, is associated with the human organization, and that it is controlled and directed by the intelligence of the medium. He adds : ' That it is the result of an *unconscious* action of the brain, the ganglion, or the nerves, will probably be deemed by those who have closely noted the phenomena to be sufficiently established.' "

"You say the medium employed was not a professional one ?" asked the banker.

" No. She was the wife of one of the members of the general committee, of high professional and social standing. She had never witnessed any of the phenomena with others, and had discovered their production in her own person by chance."

"Did she admit that the intelligence exercised was her own ?"

"No. The theory is that, as the physical phenomena were independent of her will and control, so was the exercise of the intelligence. I think a long step toward an explanation of this is in the ' Unconscious Action of the

Brain,' so ably elucidated by Dr. William B. Carpenter and
Frances Power Cobbe. The latter, in an article entitled
'Unconscious Cerebration,' which originally appeared in
Macmillan's Magazine, says, 'The phenomena with which
we are concerned have been often referred to by meta-
physicians, Leibnitz and Sir W. Hamilton amongst others,
under the name of "Latent thought" and "Preconscious activity of the soul." Dr. Carpenter, who has discovered the
physiological explanation of them, and reduced them to
harmony with other phenomena of the nervous system, has
given to them the title of "Unconscious Cerebration." The
idea is, that the brain acts without our consciousness, as is
illustrated : First. In many of our most familiar habits,
such as walking to an accustomed place of business, which
we not infrequently do, when we had, at the start, determined to go somewhere else. Again, in the case of absent-
minded people, who unconsciously say what they think of
each other, when they consciously intend to be extremely
flattering. The mind at times acts with great method and
intelligence when the subject is asleep, and the cases are
not few where difficult mathematical problems and intricate
legal questions have been solved by persons in such conditions. Another illustration of this is in recalling apparently forgotten names. We may strive for many minutes to
recall a name with which we have been familiar, and finally
cease the effort and turn our attention elsewhere ; when in
a short time, presto ! it flashes upon us. The brain, without our realization, has been at work hunting it up in the
storehouse of memory, and, being found, communicates it
to the consciousness. These things, from their comparative
familiarity, attract little attention, and yet, in view of the
limited knowledge we have had, and still have, of the action of the mind, they are wonderful in the extreme, and

it is remarkable that the ever-convenient 'spirit agency'
has not been called in to explain them.'

"Having referred to these and many other psychological
facts illustrative of 'unconscious cerebration,' Miss Cobbe
proceeds to quote, slightly abridged, from Dr. Carpenter:

"All parts of the nervous system appear to possess certain powers of automatic action. The *spinal cord* has for
primary functions the performance of the motions of res-
piration and swallowing. The automatic action of the
sensory ganglia seems to be connected with movements of
protection—such as the closing of the eyes to a flash of
light—and their secondary use enables a man to shrink from
dangers of collisions etc., before he has time for conscious
escape. Finally we arrive at the automatic action of the
cerebrum ; and here Dr. Carpenter reminds us that instead
of being (as formerly supposed) the centre of the whole
system, in direct connection with the organs of sense and
the muscular apparatus, the cerebrum is, according to
modern physiology,

"A superadded organ the development of which seems to bear a
pretty constant relation to the degree in which intelligence super-
sedes instinct as a spring of action. The ganglionic matter which
is spread out upon the surface of the hemispheres and in which their
potentiality resides, is connected with the sensory tract at their base
(which is the real centre of conveyance for the sensory nerves of the
whole body) by commissural fibres, long since termed by Reid, with
sagacious foresight, ' nerves of the internal senses,' and its anatomical
relation to the sensorium is thus precisely the same as that of the
retina, which is a ganglionic expansion connected with the sensorium
by the optic nerve. Hence it may be fairly surmised : 1. That as we
only become conscious of visual impressions on the retina when their
influence has been transmitted to the central sensorium, so we only
become conscious of ideational changes in the cerebral hemispheres
when their influence has been transmitted to the same centre ; 2.
That as visual changes may take place in the retina, of which we are
unconscious, either through temporary inactivity of the sensorium
(as in sleep) or through the entire occupation of the attention in some
other direction, so may ideational changes take place in the cere-

brum, of which we may be unconscious for want of receptivity on the part of the sensorium, but of which the results may present themselves to the consciousness as ideas elaborated by an automatic process of which we have no cognizance."

"As the result of the investigations, much more fully stated and illustrated than herein, the following powers and faculties are credited to the unconscious brain, in Miss Cobbe's article :

"1. It not only *remembers* as much as the conscious self can recall, but often much more. It is even doubtful whether it may not be capable, under certain conditions, of reproducing every impression ever made upon the senses during life.

"2. It can understand what words or things are sought to be remembered, and hunt them up, through some recondite process known only to itself, till it discovers and pounces on them.

"3. It can fancy the most beautiful pictures, and also the most terrible ones, and weave ten thousand fables with inexhaustible invention.

"4. It can perform the exceedingly difficult task of mental arrangement and logical division of subjects.

"5. It can transact all the mechanical business of walking, reading, writing, sewing, playing, etc. etc.

"6. It can tell the hour in the middle of the night without a time-piece."

"And to what does all this tend ?" said the merchant.

"Simply this," responded the angular young man, "that in the unconscious action of the brain, of which we are just beginning to obtain some knowledge—may, no doubt, be found the secret of the 'intelligence' manifested in the physical phenomena referred to ; and farther, that in the indestructible memory, acting with or forming part of such unconscious action, may be found a solution for all the mental phenomena which have been observed in so-called spiritualism. How often do we hear from its votaries, 'I had not thought of such a person or such an incident for years,' in the presence of the clairvoyant or medium who, to his astonishment, has called it up to him. And this is true, as far as conscious thought is concerned ; but who can tell to what extent the brain has dwelt upon such person or incident, in its unconscious activity, and which has, in its mysterious workings, communicated the thought to another mind ?"

"I think the solution of those phenomena can be much more easily explained," said the merchant, "and that it lies in the fact that the medium or clairvoyant has obtained the knowledge from some extraneous source."

"I grant you that in the very great majority of instances."

While this attempted elucidation of the causes of phenomena had been going on, another gentleman had entered the office. He was pale, of thoughtful mien, and having a wealth of black hair and whiskers. He had quietly seated himself and listened, with much apparent interest. As the angular young man finished, another, who had not as yet spoken, arose with an impatient air, and as he walked the floor, exclaimed, "Let us be reasonable! What is the use of all these fine-spun theories based on nothing ? It is not difficult to ascertain certain facts. I will open the way if you have any desire to investigate this matter. Media are not frauds or humbugs. Yes, I am a Spiritualist, and am content in so being. Media are the means through which our departed friends communicate with us. They stand between the living and the dead, and not even the frequency of such communications can rid them of the feeling of awe and reverence which their occult, unexplainable powers induce within them. I have been a Spiritualist for two years. It has convinced me that the soul is immortal, that I shall live in my individuality hereafter ; that with others, my friends here, I shall wander 'on the banks of that eternal river.' Spiritualism furnishes to us our only assurance of such existence hereafter. It shows us that we enter the new life as we leave the old one ; that the affections and interests of this life, the love of humanity for a time retain us here, but the tendency is onward and upward toward fountains of eternal happiness. I have witnessed manifestations which are inexplicable on the base of any other theory than that of an intelligent entity outside of both medium and his visitor, and which the theories of psychic force and unconscious cerebration, concerning which the writers on those subjects seem to know little, though allowed every thing that is claimed for them, can not account for. I have been furnished information of which I never had any knowledge, and of which the medium could not, in the nature of things, by any possibility have known. It is not a difficult thing to test this matter. There are plenty of media in the city. Go to them for information which you desire, and you will soon be convinced."

"Let us be calm," said a broker.

"I have many friends who are Spiritualists," said the banker, "and they have often endeavored to prevail upon me to visit a spiritual medium and try to obtain some knowledge of the circumstances surrounding my father's death, who, as you all know, was murdered some years since. My brother and partner here, and myself have labored, regardless of trouble or expense, to find some clue to the murderer, and while I have little confidence——"

"Go to such medium as I direct," said the believer in Spiritualism, "and I guarantee you will ascertain what you want to know."

"You had better stay away," said the new-comer, " and

save your money, to continue your efforts by earthly means."

"I judge you are not a Spiritualist," said the broker.

"No, sir! Not a Spiritualist in any sense whatever. I have listened with much interest to your remarks in relation to this subject of Spiritualism, and, as it is one to which I have given considerable attention, I would like to make a few observations in regard to it."

"Couldn't you write them out, and submit them at some future day?" inquired the elegantly-dressed young man, with an expression of anxiety.

"Certainly," said the new-comer, somewhat abashed, "if you desire to——"

"Let us be serious," said the banker. "Go on!"

The new-comer, after looking around with an inquiring expression, continued, "I am an adherent of that system of thought and life elaborated by Auguste Comte, and known as Positivism."

"Allow me to form your acquaintance!" exclaimed the angular young man. "To my shame be it said, I know nothing of Positivism, probably owing to the fact that my tendencies are all toward Orthodoxy. Tell us something about it."

New-comer. "It claims to be an integral doctrine, giving a complete explanation of the world, of man, his duty and destiny. It rejects completely all forms of theological and metaphysical belief; in other words, all forms of supernaturalism. The true positive spirit consists in substituting the study of the invariable laws of phenomena for that of their so-called causes, whether proximate or primary; in a word, in studying the 'How' instead of the 'Why.' The principle of theology is to explain every thing by supernatural wills."

Believer. "Then you are an Atheist; at least, I am unable to distinguish between Atheism and Positivism."

New-comer. "Your inability to make the distinction arises from the want of due appreciation of the exact grounds in dispute. The Atheist is, at bottom, a theologian; he does not reject the problems of theology; he merely rejects the solution of those problems, and in so doing he is extremely illogical. So long as the mind continues to perplex itself with the problems, there is no better explanation possible than the one spontaneously given, that they proceed from supernatural will or wills. Positivists, on the other hand, reject the problem on the ground that it is utterly inaccessible to the intellect. Moral considerations make it imperative on us to study the laws of phenomena, instead of wasting our strength in a vain search for first or final causes."

Angular Young Man. "If this doctrine is what you represent it to be, it should afford an explanation of this wide-spread delusion of Spiritualism."

New-comer. "To give an exhaustive exposition of it, from a Positive point of view, would perhaps tax your patience to an extent to which you would hardly submit. It would certainly do nothing toward settling the question whether the media are deceivers or deceived. And though this be decided, it would fall far short of accomplishing the overthrow of this disease or seriously affecting its career."

Believer, (*indignantly.*) "I would like to know on what grounds you characterize Spiritualism as a disease."

New-comer. "Perhaps a sufficient evidence that it is so, might be found in a study of the mental and physical conditions of the great mass of its votaries. But I will try to make an explanation of this statement, and in order to do so, we must first understand what we mean by health and disease. The popular notions on this subject are wholly

metaphysical ; health and disease are regarded as entities.
The popular language at once betrays the existing intellectual fallacies. 'He caught a cold,' 'He caught a fever,'
etc., show that colds and fevers are regarded as tangible
entities. Now, the scientific explanation of health is this :
'Health is the result of the harmonious action of all the
organs of the body,' and the complete combination of all
the bodily functions is the condition or unity thus termed.
Disease, on the other hand, results when this unity or harmony is disturbed by the excess or defect of an organ to
discharge its legitimate and normal functions. This disturbance may proceed either from without or from within,
when the normal limits of variation are exceeded, in a plus
or minus direction, by the prolonged action, either of the
environment or of the organism. Now, this definition can
be extended and applied to our emotional life as well as our
physical life. All the phenomena of life, whether of the
individual or of society, are comprised in three grand divisions : Thought, feeling, and activity. How to bring
these into harmonious relations, is the problem of modern
philosophy."

Merchant. " How do you apply this to Spiritualism ?"

New-comer. " To do this, we must take a comprehensive
view of society ; not alone as it exists to-day, because to
understand the age in which we live, we must study it in
relation to all preceding ages. To the student of history,
few events afford such material for speculation as the spread
of epidemic delusions, especially religious delusions, and
history is replete with them. A critical examination enables us to see how they may be accounted for, when the
definition of health, above given, is extended so as to em-
brace our mental, moral, and social life."

Broker. " I can't understand how such palpable absurdities can be accepted by sensible men."

New-comer. " The difference between tweedle-dee and tweedle-dum is much greater, perhaps, than at first sight we are disposed to think. Religious dogmas do not rest on reason. For example, how much rationality is there in the dogmas of the conception of Christ, the Trinity, and Transubstantiation, if submitted to the tests of physiology, mathematics, and chemistry ? I undertake to say that the vagaries of Spiritualism do not surpass these eminently respectable beliefs in absurdity."

Believer. " I don't see that you have made out that Spiritualism is a disease."

New-comer. " Let me continue, again directing your attention to the great divisions of the individual and of the social life—thought, feeling, and activity. Any undue variation of any one of these will produce moral and social disorders. Now, when we consider that in the mass the intellect is extremely feeble compared with the feelings, we can readily understand how delusions, under certain conditions, do take possession of the minds of men. We all know that epidemic diseases can be traced to physical causes existing in the environment, and their disastrous effects are greatly enhanced when the epidemic produces a panic which takes the imagination captive. History shows us that periods of great physical suffering, caused by famine, pestilence, earthquakes, and other unusual phenomena, are prolific sources of mental disorders. In these cases, the intellect and the emotions are thrown out of their normal relations by physical causes. At other times, the disturbance proceeds from within. The destruction of the world and other startling notions have from time to time taken possession of Western Europe and thrown the nations into disorder. As to mental disorders, there are two causes from whence they proceed : First, the exciting cause ; next, the predisposing cause ; the one objective, the other subjective. Now, let us apply this to modern Spiritualism. In this case, the exciting cause was primarily the old theological belief in the existence of spirits, roused into unusual activity by the strange phenomena known as the 'Rochester Knockings,' and the predisposing cause was the prevailing rationalism which, since the inaugura-tion of the scientific era by Galileo, has been going on at an ever-increasing rapidity. If you examine the mental condition of Spiritualists, you will find they repudiate with contempt all the old theological dogmas. They are (in spirit at least) in a state of war with all the traditions of the past, and nearly all existing social institutions. They are destructives, pure and simple."

Believer. "Yes, and we will ultimately inaugurate a new era of freedom and progress."

New-comer. "I do not share that hope. Spiritualism is destructive, not constructive. A glance at its present con-dition does not warrant any such conclusion as you men-tion. It has no well-defined purpose or object. It is utterly destitute of the means by which to accomplish a reorganization. Its whole scope and tendency is divergent, not convergent. It rests on a vague sentimentalism. It claims to be a new revelation for the healing of the nations, a religion with millions of adherents, and yet it does not own a decent roof under which to worship. It claims to be the advocate of science, education, and morality. It has founded neither a library, college, nor school. It has neither a philosophy nor a polity. Its literature is a strange jumble of metaphysical jargon, extracted from the limbo of worn-out creeds. Its most ardent supporters are doubtful of the faith which is within them, and only strive to convince others, that their own convictions may be strengthened. Its doctrines are evolved from the individual consciousness of its members, and the one is as various as the other is numerous. Judging from its effects, their faith is out of harmony with a proper performance of the duties of this life, and they are useful members of society much in proportion as they are derelict in their worship at the new shrine. Fortunately for the welfare of society, it has no elements of coherence ; otherwise its anarchical and revolutionary aims and tendencies would greatly endanger its safety. In criticising it thus harshly, but (I trust) justly, I distinctly disclaim any intention to wantonly assail those who hold this belief. As far as my observation goes—and it has been somewhat extensive—they are better than their creed. They are very generally found on the side of freedom and justice. They have the welfare of humanity sincerely at heart. I do not condemn them, only their faith.

"Our special scientists are greatly to blame for the attitude they have assumed in regard to this subject. They have shown themselves to be wholly destitute of their true social function by prejudging this matter and treating it with contempt. Happily, they are at last beginning to show some appreciation of their mission by devoting some attention to this subject. Say what you will, there is an enormous amount of testimony in favor of the existence of phenomena of an occult nature which is not included in the domain of science. But that these phenomena can be made to constitute the basis of a new religion is a sad commentary on those who direct the spiritual forces of Christendom. That millions of men and women, many of whom have received the highest culture our institutions of learning afford, can cast aside the faith of their ancestors, and find consolation for their souls in such a degrading superstition as this modern Spiritualism, shows conclusively how inadequate the popular theology must be to satisfy the spiritual needs of the time."

A thoughtful silence followed this elucidation of Spiri-

tualism in the light of Positivism, which the elegantly-
dressed young man broke by the exclamation, "Are we
going to dine?"

"I have never visited any of these media," said the merchant, "and I suggest that we make up a party and witness
some of the manifestations." This was agreed upon.

In carrying out this suggestion, a number of visits were
made to different media. The two bankers, (who were
brothers,) as has been intimated, had heard numerous stories
in reference to the wonderful knowledge manifested by the
media, and the information which they at times afforded
applicants, so well authenticated as to stagger their unbe-
lief; and having at heart the intensest desire to learn of
the manner and means of their father's death, determined
to consult the media, carefully complying with every prescribed condition, in the bare hope that something might
come of it. After visiting several, and submitting their
questions, they observed that the answers received were all
of the most general character, affording no clue whatever
to the information sought; that the responses from the respective media were often directly contradictory, always
inconsistent, only agreeing in this, that the "spirit," for
some reason, could not give the required information at
present, but would do so on some future occasion, an incident of which was coming again and paying another five
dollars to the medium. After a variety of experiments,
made by these and others of the seven gentlemen mentioned, all tending to show that the pretenses of the media
had no good foundation, it was determined to go to work
and ascertain if these manifestations could not be accounted
for without the agency of spirits. And so "the Committee"
was constituted.

A few words more in detail in reference to the *personnel.*
One was a Spiritualist, made so, as he said, by the unac-

countable manifestations he had witnessed. The others, of various temperaments and habit of thought, agreeing in this, that they were not inclined to refer unexplained phenomena to supernatural agency. Two were for twenty years merchants in this city, and for the past ten years have been engaged in a general banking business. One of these, from a boy, had been an adept at sleight-of-hand tricks, and had a variety of weird accomplishments with which he entertained his friends. A habit of looking into all such tricks, in order to discover the manner of their performance, had made him very acute therein, and it was his boast that no one of them could be repeated a certain number of times in his presence without his discovering it. Both the brothers were keen judges of human nature, and not accustomed to being imposed upon. Two were gold brokers, not reverential, but, as required in their profession, sharp, eager, watchful. The fifth, a well-known lumber merchant, of impassive face and great acumen. Of the believer, a word further. He was impassioned and earnest, full of reasons for the faith that was in him ; a rationalist in this, that he must have something tangible, or seemingly so, as a base for belief. The seventh was a journalist.

And here let us pause and consider. Above all things, let us be just, as, with much respect for Solomon, we are speaking of something new under the sun. A journalist, and accustomed to looking at human nature from that stand-point, not always a flattering one. Serene forever. Impudent if you please, from confidence in the strength of the "third estate" at his back. Not approving of "interviews," as calculated to bore both parties, but ready to visit Lucifer himself with pertinacity and equanimity if required. Knowing no difference in men in his presence, whether from social, intellectual, or political position ; all one before the impersonation of the great people—which he is—and so accustomed to speaking evil of dignitaries ; claiming to know all science and all knowledge ; at least ready to talk and write learnedly and exhaustively of them ; from long habit discovering pinchbeck at once as though by an enchanter's wand, yet not caring to talk about it, satisfied with the conscious superiority of knowing ; the equal of senators and thieves, regretting that the line of demarkation, in these latter days, is so finely drawn, thus giving less scope to his talents ; having every accomplishment or the power of affecting them ; a statesman, politician, lawyer, and theologian ; a man about town and of society ; harmonizing with the most luxurious mansion and not incongruous with the surroundings of a hovel ; a diner-out and a wit ; a charm in the domestic circle ; at home in the club or a corner grocery. In short, something modern. An American and a journalist, evolving from his innate consciousness that there are humbugs in the world.

These gentlemen became early convinced that " Spiritualism," as a faith or a creed, is not in harmony with a proper performance of the duties of this life. Supposed intercourse with the beings of another world makes its votaries careless of this. They seem to reason, " What matter what ye shall eat, or what ye shall drink, or wherewithal be clothed, since we are so soon to be with those who have no need of these ?" and so wait, longing and useless. They saw many with fortunes spent, families broken and separated, business ruined, energies wasted, and, being humanitarians, desired to do away with a delusion. This formed a strong incentive to investigation.

CHARLATANISM.

CHAPTER II.

THOUGH in the course of the investigation many visits were made to some of the media mentioned, I shall, for the most part, confine myself to but one interview with them respectively, as a sample of the whole, though giving, at the same time, the conclusions we arrived at from all the sittings accorded us, and shall refer to the individuals composing "the Committee" only when necessary to a due understanding of what took place.

After consulting with our Spiritualist friend, who was acquainted with all the more prominent media of the city, and who was so certain of our ultimate conversion that he gladly undertook to introduce us, when necessary, into all the charmed circles where spirits from the vasty deep and other localities most do congregate, we determined to visit those considered the most convincing first.

J. V. MANSFIELD.

We therefore selected J. V. Mansfield, "test-medium," who, according to his advertisement in the *Banner of Light*, answers sealed letters, at 361 Sixth avenue, New-York. Terms, $5 and four three-cent stamps. Arriving at the house, we were shown into a bright, cheerful-looking room on the second floor, fronting the avenue. Having no taste for upholstery, I do not describe the furniture further than to say that a small table, covered with paper and papers, occupied such relative position to the window as to receive the best possible light from it. We found the medium a well-preserved man of sixty, with black hair, combed directly back from the forehead. He received us with a courtesy bordering on *bonhomie*, and our attention was almost immediately turned to a very museum of curiosities which the room contained. He informed us that he had been a medium for spirit communication for more than twenty years, had traveled in every part of the globe, and, having a taste for curiosities, had collected those we saw around us, oftentimes at great expense, trouble, and *finesse*. He cheerfully remarked that he allowed nothing to stand in the way of obtaining possession of any thing in that line he took a fancy to—a statement we readily accepted—and he recounted to us one or two anecdotes illustrative of his capacity for appropriating which were quite entertaining. Some ten or fifteen minutes passed in this way. Those whose task it was to watch him clearly perceived that he was on the alert every moment, keen, attentive, and ready to catch at any straw indicative of character or expressive of a fact. He naturally manifested no impatience and made no reference to business. When asked if he could give any manifestations, he did not know ; he could never tell ; as far as he could judge, the conditions were favorable. If we desired it, he would try. "However, spirits like mortals demand conditions," he said, " and without these, no manifestations can be had." While it would be a matter of indifference how many were present, if all were in harmonious relation, it was so difficult to find this in more than two persons that he had established a rule that no more than that number should be present. This had been anticipated, and all save the appointed two with meekness and solemnity took their departure. He then requested one of the visitors to sit at the table, upon

which were some long strips of thin, transparent paper, write
a question addressed to some deceased person, sign it with
the writer's name, fold it over in a prescribed manner, which
left three or four thicknesses of paper outside of the writing.
This was done, the question being written by the banker,
addressed to the spirit of his father, asking how many persons were concerned in his murder, and how much a certain
gentleman, still living, was indebted to him when he died.
It was handed to the medium, who seated himself and began manipulating, rubbing it with his hand, running out
his tongue meanwhile, twitching convulsively at intervals
without seeming result. He finally stated that perhaps he
required a little more magnetism, and asked to hold the
hand of the writer a moment. Immediately thereafter his
arms began to shake rapidly, he rolled the paper into a much
smaller compass, seized a brush from a mucilage-bottle, and
pasted it together so that it could only be subsequently
opened by destroying most of the paper. He then began to
write with his right hand, his left index-finger meanwhile
keeping up a constant tapping, not unlike the ticking of a
telegraphic instrument, which he said indicated the response.
He did not explain how ; probably not to the ear, as he subsequently claimed to be entirely ignorant of what his hand
wrote. An examination of the answer thus written showed
that it indicated a knowledge of the question, but gave no
clue to the information asked, save it stated that there were
three persons engaged in the murder. The " spirit " could
not tell how much the gentleman referred to owed him
when he died, but promised to investigate and respond in
the future. Whether this was to be done by consulting the
ghosts of dead papers and of records long since passed into
the maw of worms, or otherwise, did not appear. Farther,
and in general terms, the spirit of the father was present,
was happy to communicate with son ; couldn't "manifest "

much, as control of medium not good ; happy to see son interested in great truths of Spiritualism, and hoped would continue investigations. Would communicate more freely next time. The other visitor was then requested to write a question, which he did and in the same manner, addressing it to the spirit of his brother, and asking concerning a favorite cousin. The answer came back pertinent, and, as the questioner glanced at it, he became very much affected, and hastened to the window with his back to the others, and remained there some time in a profound agitation.

"What did you write, doctor ?" asked his friend.

"I have no idea," was the response. "I never know what I write when controlled by the spirits. He seems very much affected."

"Very much."

The gentleman eventually recovered his equanimity, and the two took their leave. On their way down-town, they stepped into the respective places of business of the supposed deceased brother and cousin, and obtained a verbal certificate from them that they were not dead and had not been. The former admitted that he had been out of spirits during the morning, and even then had not a large stock on hand ; but he was certain his spirit had not been out of him. A knowledge that his brother and cousin, from whom he was receiving communications as departed spirits, were alive and well, accounted for his agitation while in the rooms of the medium. Subsequent visits to Mansfield were made by different members of "the Committee," with the same or similar results. Our questions were invariably addressed to living or fictitious persons, notwithstanding which their accommodating spirits were always at hand and in responsive humor. On one occasion, deceived by a pet name, the spirit informed us that a person we desired to communicate with was a darling little "angel in the ' Celestial sphere,'" whereas in reality she is in 210 pounds of "earth-form," and the happy mother of numerous offspring. Answers from his sister were given to a gentleman who never had a sister, and from his brother to another who never had a brother. At different times, every member of " the Committee" was complimented on the amount of " magnetism" which his organism contained, and assured that he would eventually become a medium of rare power. In no single instance was a particle of desired information obtained, even when " the conditions" were strictly complied with ; and it soon became evident that the only thing to account for was how a knowledge of the question was obtained. After closely watching the medium—who, by the way, from long habit, has a thousand scarcely noticeable means of distracting the attention—the manipulation and rubbing of the paper, a study of the "conditions," the situation of the table with reference to the light in the fore and background, the style of paper and the soft pencil furnished the visitor, and the fact that the medium invariably rolled up the paper containing the question in much smaller compass before answering, and pasted it together with much mucilage, thus rendering an immediate examination of it impossible—the conclusion was reached that the question was read through the paper. An experiment under similar conditions demonstrated that this could be done with the greatest ease—an ease which rendered it wonderful that any body could have been deceived thereby. One of " the Committee," of whom Mr. Mansfield and subsequently other media stated, " He has wonderful mediumistic powers," at once began "to develop," and, by himself, and with the aid of his honest and sagacious associates, soon had manifestations which were declared by prominent Spiritualists to be the most convincing they had ever seen, though they had been twenty-five years investigating the subject. But of this more hereafter. Believing that the slightest inkling of our design would prevent any further interviews with Mansfield, and that the extent of his manifestations would be in proportion to our apparent gullibility, we made no question of his genuineness, and accepted them as wonderful, if not supernatural.

Though, at this time, fully satisfied that the "manifestations," not only of this medium but of others, were the result of fraud and chicanery, such had been the wonderful stories told us, we were doubtful of our ability to get at all the tricks of the media. I remark, *en passant*, herein we did ourselves an injustice. They proved very simple. Very greatly inferior to the ordinary tricks of the necromancers. We had no difficulty. But, thus believing, we determined to take Mr. Mansfield into our confidence, explain our appreciation of his "little game," and endeavor to induce him, in the interest of humanity, to assist us. I regret to say we misjudged him. He was obdurate. To the desired end, four of "the Committee" called on him in a body. He received us without suspicion, answered some questions, getting at the contents of the paper in a manner now so clearly perceptible that a maintenance of gravity was difficult. One of "the Committee" then quietly remarked to him, "Doctor, we have discovered your trick, and we think it a good one." Twenty years of practice in deceit had given this man a marvelous power of self-control, and yet for an instant, and in spite of himself, there swept athwart his face an expression which was the best evidence of the truth of our charge ; such as only the realization that the results of a lifetime of labor were about to be swept away, could produce. He recovered in an instant, however, and exclaimed, "You do not mean to say this is a trick ?"

"Certainly," was the response ; "we have got it, and can do it as well as you can."

"Let me see you do it then."

" Sit down at your table and write a question, complying with your own conditions."

He seated himself and wrote, taking particular care to go wide of the conditions he himself prescribed, making the paper much narrower and so folding it that the writing was in the crease, and, being reminded of this, refused to proceed. He was then informed that we had no desire to make war upon him, but we were determined to get at the various tricks of the media, and wanted him to assist us. For a time he was undecided, and it was evident he was puzzling his brain as to the best course to pursue. He finally asked,

"What do you wish me to do ?"

" We want you to help us to get Slade's and Foster's tricks."

" I am willing to do any thing to expose fraud, but I can not get a sitting with either Slade or Foster. They are not friendly to me. I would go on my hands and knees to Slade's house to find out the 'slate-writing.' "

"Oh ! I reckon you can get it, doctor."

By this time he had made up his mind, and resolved to defy us. "I tell you, gentlemen," he said, " you are all wrong ; this is no trick, and if you can do it, you are mediums."

Seeing farther effort would be useless, we arose to leave, when he said, "Gentlemen, I must be paid for my time."

" O doctor !" said the banker, "you don't intend to charge us for this sitting. I would advise you not." He persisted, and, on being informed that we would not submit to the swindle without attempting redress, he defiantly exclaimed, " Do your worst, gentlemen; those who believe will continue to, and those who do not will disbelieve none the more." Ten dollars were given him, and we left him with his trick literally so transparent that a second-rate juggler would despise it ; left him to gloat over the weakness of human

nature, and to trade on the tenderest emotions of the human
soul.

"DR." HENRY SLADE.

The attention of the committee had meanwhile been at-
tracted to Dr. Henry Slade, located at 210 West Forty-
third street, who is styled a clairvoyant physician, and gives
"physical manifestations," ostensibly from spirits. This
man's reputation is very high among the Spiritualists. He
is by them regarded as the test medium *par excellence*, and
to him is the doubting, inquiring mind led, that every cloud
of suspicion may be removed and the trembling neophyte,
awe-struck in the presence of the supernatural, may be ini-
tiated into the glorious light of modern spiritual philosophy.
And yet the doctor's tricks are very simple, easily discovered, and easily explained. "The Committee," in one or two
sittings, albeit he was extremely suspicious, and doled out
to them only a limited portion of the manifestations with
which he entertains credulous believers, discovered the whole
thing ; though, as with every medium, the conditions which
his attendant spirits prescribe are precisely those which best
aid deception. The conclusions which I mention in my description of an interview are such as "the Committee" arrived
at after several visits, as the same manifestations were given
and the same course of treatment pursued toward every
applicant. On arriving at the house, the visitor is ushered
into a reception-room by the medium's coadjutor and facto-
tum—a flashy-appearing individual, with something of the air
of a ring-master of a circus. It is clearly the task of this
man to take the measure of the caller and to judge how extensive a dose can be administered with safety. This he
does by a few well-turned questions and a keen examination
of the physiognomy and style of address. He then leaves
the room to ascertain if the doctor can be seen, and after a
time sufficient to communicate all that is needed, he returns

and reports the results. If any suspicions are entertained, the medium can see no one. Otherwise the visitor is requested to walk up-stairs. Here the doctor appears in person : no aged professor with wand in hand summoning spirits from a great variety of places, but a tall, slim young man of perhaps thirty-five years, arrayed in dressing-gown and hair whose elaborateness of curl is suggestive of the barber rather than nature. His manner is not impressive, and with all his practice he has not yet learned to appear at ease. The visitor, if calling for the first time, is compelled to undergo another examination here, before being admitted into the sanctum sanctorum. Several questions as to his residence and business are asked him, and if he volunteers a remark, is listened to with deference and encouraged to talk, evidently that some clue to his character may be obtained.

"I painted that picture when in a trance," says the doctor, pointing to a portrait in oil over the mantel. "I never painted a line in my life when in a normal condition," he adds. When making this remark, his eye is intently fixed on the visitor, possibly that he may judge how much credence is given to this wonderful story, that he may shape his course accordingly. It is seldom that more than one person at a time is admitted, and then only in case of believers, who, accepting the manifestations as genuine, will not be likely to scrutinize too closely. Entering an adjoining room, neatly though rather scantily furnished, and presenting an air of comfort, the medium removes the cloth from a table in the centre, and requests the visitor to examine it. It is a plain black-walnut table, with leaves, not differing from other tables, insomuch as the doctor's tricks do not require that it should. His specialty is "slate-writing," so-called, or obtaining communications written by the spirits on a slate. One of these articles is produced, and the caller is requested to "examine that slate, sir." This he does, and finds nothing on either side of it. If the medium intends to show a certain manifestation hereinafter mentioned, he takes the slate in his hand and walks to the corner of the room, returning at once. This is done as though incidentally, and with no definite object, and generally it is not noticed. Seating himself at the table on the side where the leaf is raised, he places his visitor to his right with the legs of the table inclosing him. He then bites a small bit from a pencil lying near, and places it on the slate; this is for the use of the spirits. The next step is to place the caller in such position that he can see nothing under the table. This is accomplished by requesting him to cross his hands in the centre of the table and covering them with his own hand. In this position he waits for the necessary "magnetism." It will be perceived that the breast of the visitor is brought close against the edge of the table, and as he is thus held during the sitting, he has no opportunity to see the operations of the medium's right hand, his legs and feet beneath. The slate held in the right hand of the medium begins moving to and fro, which is attributed to the spirits. After a time, the medium asks, "Will the spirits write?" Three raps against the leg of the table are heard and again under the heel of the medium, indicating, "We will." The slate is forced with great violence against the table near the edge, the medium making apparent efforts to force it up against the leaf, which is finally accomplished. A sound of writing is heard, and after a few moments the slate is brought out. If, after the examination of the slate by the visitor, the doctor walked to the corner of the room as described, a long and well-written communication from some spirit, generally that of his deceased wife, as he states, appears upon it. If, on the contrary, he did not go to the corner, only a few marks are found on the slate, bearing some resemblance to writing, and which the medium deciphers to suit himself.

" I can read it because I am accustomed to it," he naively remarks. It must be borne in mind that the writing is on that
side of the slate which is seemingly close against the under
side of the table, and the visitor who has seen it placed in
that position with no writing upon it sees it withdrawn
with the hieroglyphics upon it, and is mystified. As this is
his most important and convincing manifestation, and the
only one at all difficult to understand, which he would show
the members of " the Committee," I may as well stop here and
explain. And first let me say that all the demonstrations
by the medium, in rapping the slate against the table in the
violent manner described, his apparent endeavors to get it
in proper position against the lower side of the table, followed, when it is once there, by a sound as of a pencil writing, are
made after the communication is written. The success of
the trick is in leading the spectator to believe the writing is
in progress when in fact it has been accomplished previously. When the medium goes to the corner of the room, after the visitor has examined the slate, he returns with another slate upon which the long and well-written communication has been previously prepared. In no single instance
has a second communication of any length been written, or
one in a legible hand, the medium remaining at the table.
The long dressing-gown he wears and a limited knowledge
of sleight of hand render this change very easy. The few
words of unskillful writing in which the later communications,
invariably consisting of a few words, are couched, are written with a grain of pencil similar to those placed on the top
of the slate in the presence of the sitter, lying on the finger
of the medium and against the lower side of the slate, and
this is done during the time the slate is moving to and fro
while the medium has his left hand upon the crossed hands
of the visitor in the centre of the table, waiting for " magnetism." As the slate is about to be withdrawn, by another

motion which is "quicker than sight," it is turned as it is
brought out, and the credulous spectator is certain the same
side is presented to him which was against the table. This
was evidenced to "the Committee" on several occasions by
marks on the respective sides of the slate, which, being closely watched, showed that one side went under and the other
came out. The members of "the Committee" were often assured by Slade's supporters that the writing was done upon
the top of the table. To one of these a considerable sum,
to be devoted to distressed mediums, was offered if Slade
would do this in the presence of any one of our number. A
sitting was obtained, and the doctor was informed of what
was desired. "Oh! yes; that has often been done," he said.
"I don't know how the conditions are. Probably if you
come for just that thing, you will not get it. The spirits do
as they choose, and will not be dictated to. However, I will
try." An application was made to the spirits, who, being in
an obliging humor, rapped out an affirmative by using the
medium's knee against the table. This was highly satisfactory, and much interest was manifested. The two were
seated at the table as before described, and the slate in the
doctor's right hand began moving here and there, under the
table, as usual, and the doctor began writing with his fin-
gers as usual, too. He made several efforts to get the slate
on the table, but without success. As he was about to suc-
ceed and release it from his hand, the visitor exclaimed,
"Turn it over, doctor! I can see there is no writing on this
side now." "I will," was the response, but he didn't. He
shot the slate across the room, and going to pick it up returned and said, "You see there is no writing on either side."
That was true, but the finger-marks where he had rubbed
the writing off when he picked it up were plainly visible.
The attempt thus proving a failure, it was not repeated.

He then stated that he was suffering very much from

worriment of mind, owing to sickness in his family, which prevented his giving satisfactory manifestations. He was all " unstrung," and should not sit again for several days. The two gentlemen then withdrew. As we were satisfied that no farther manifestations would be given us, and with a view of ascertaining how much this " worriment," which prevented his sittings, was real, within an hour after his statement that he would give no more sittings, a slim-built, thoughtful-looking young man, with long hair, residing in a country village near Albany, might be seen ringing the door-bell of the famous test-medium, Dr. Slade. The door, as usual, was opened by the obliging Simmons, of whom he inquired, " Is this Dr. Slade ?"

" No, sir ! but walk in."

Ushered into the reception-room, he was asked if he desired to see Dr. Slade.

Yes ! As he happened to be in the city, and his friends at home were much interested in the subject of Spiritualism, he had called, hoping to see some manifestations ; but perhaps the doctor——

" Retain your seat. Where do you reside ?"

" Near Albany."

" Have you seen any spiritual manifestations ?"

" Well, some. We have our circles at home, and the table sometimes moves, and the raps are heard, but nothing further. We have read of Dr. Slade in the *Banner of Light*, and——"

" Excuse me a moment, and I will see if the doctor is disengaged."

The thoughtful-looking young man retained his seat and soon Simmons returned and requested him to walk up-stairs, which he did. He was met at the top by the doctor, who requested him to walk into the parlor, to which he assented without remonstrance. He mentioned his name and was invited to sit.

"I called, doctor," he said, "in hopes to see some manifestations; but I am aware——"

"Have you seen any manifestations?"

"Some few. I am not much inclined to believe in such things; but my friends wanted me to call, and if——"

"Walk into the other room."

He did so, looking around with a certain solemn gravity as he entered. The doctor removed the cloth from the table, and requested him to examine it.

"O doctor! I am sure I have no idea! Pardon me! It is rather a delicate——"

"Oh! I think nothing of that. Examine it."

He did so in a very cursory way, and seated himself as requested in a chair to the right of the doctor. A slate was then produced and examined. It was chipped in one corner of each side, and in a different manner, which the thoughtful young man perceived, and which enabled him to verify the fact that the slate was turned on being placed under the table. The manifestations of slate-writing which followed need not be referred to, as they were in no way different from those already described. That the explanation heretofore given is correct was easily seen. At this time, the medium began to see lights in various parts of the room, now hovering over the back of a chair, now on the wall, again forming a halo around the head of the young man, who felt flattered, but was not otherwise impressed. He remained passive, not having much confidence in his ability to see these lights, as the spirits had declared previously that he was not a medium, and only after the doctor repeated, "Look there! there! don't you see it?" several times, did he turn his head. Some manifestations—such as the tipping of the table by the doctor's foot or rapping with his knee—invariably followed. A small accordeon was then produced, and, after it was examined by the visitor, the spirits were asked if they would play on it, and they rapped "yes." The hands were again crossed on the table, and the medium, holding the instrument in his right hand, under the table, played a familiar air upon it in a very creditable manner. That he was so playing was clearly perceptible in despite of the position. The visitor's attention being again called to the light, the slide in the accordeon was thrown out and upon the table. After a few minor manifestations, such as raising the table with his leg, which as it came down unfortunately struck that of the visitor extended for that purpose, the doctor announced that he was sometimes controlled by the spirit of an Indian. This Indian, as others had been informed, died before the pale-face landed, but somehow had managed to acquire an imperfect knowledge of English, though with a peculiar objection to the nominative case. "I feel him coming now," said the doctor. A shudder or two, his eyes closed, and, extending his hand in salutation, he said, "Me Indian, me control this medium; me come see you; happy you come; your friends glad you come here; investigate Spiritualism; make them very happy; no manifestations much this time. You come again. Me control this medium, make many manifestations. Me go now. Good-by." And the medium opened his eyes. A few desultory remarks followed, the doctor stating, "We don't always get the best manifestations at the first sitting."

"Yes! so the Indian said."

Solemnly the young man rose to leave. "You will find Mr. Simmons below, who will settle with you," cheerfully remarked the doctor. Mr. Simmons was there, and took his $5, as the medium had prophesied. Three minutes after, a young man with long hair might have been seen seated in a Broadway car, whose cheerful countenance attracted the attention of the passengers opposite. Deceived by his air and language, both factotum and medium had been imposed upon, and the latter went through his entire *rôle* of tricks in so careless a manner that they were seen through without effort, and without any evidence of that worriment he had spoken of.

"DOCTOR" H. C. GORDON.

The wonderful manifestations made through this distinguished medium were early brought to the attention of " the Committee." He was one of the few who possessed the occult power, not only of calling back from the spirit-world those who had departed hence; but, such was the wonderful development of his physical organism, that out from it went an emanation, which enabled the spirit to materialize itself, and once again appear in the form and with the lineaments it had while here, only with a glorified beauty, which is of the realms where sickness and sorrow are unknown. Controlled, as was stated, by the spirits of a number of Catholic priests—the most prominent of whom was the late Bishop White—who had carried with them to another world the tastes and habits of this, the " doctor" had erected within an extension - of his parlors, at 406 Fourth avenue, an altar, over which long wax candles shed a solemn light ; within whose niches and arches stole the fragrant incense, possibly as grateful now to the good bishop, using the olfactory nerves of the medium, as when on earth he waved the censer before awe-struck, kneeling thousands. Lying in the centre was a copy of the New Testament revised by the spirits, who, it is hoped, manifested more intelligence in the revision than they have when treating of matters purely earthly ; and the walls were decorated with numerous scrolls, containing quotations from it. Other ornamentation, of the "Leo and Lotus" style, gave a pleasant if somewhat flashy aspect to the surroundings. Within it all sat the "doctor," an unpleasant spider, notwithstanding the corresponding gorgeousness of his raiment. White-haired, even to the eye-brows, and very pale, he affected a certain solemnity, eminently suggestive of unpleasant sensations in the stomach The front-parlor was devoted to visitors, at so much per head, which kept the medium going until, his great work done, he should join the souls he had so much obliged by the use of his "earth-form" while in this life. Here, as within the "holy of holies," gathered the faithful and solemn, yet collected, witnessed the "spirits" called up by the "doctor's" art. Seen in a dim light, to be sure, and through a gauze curtain which hung across the room in front of the altar, some distance from it, and yet with sufficient distinctness to enable them to recognize parents, daughters, sons, friends, whose forms stole upon the retina, with weird mystic movement, accompanied by the "doctor."

It was a good thing ; as witness the following certificate in the *Banner of Light* of January 11th, Anno Domini 1873 :

SPIRITS MATERIALIZING THEMSELVES.

A SEANCE AT DR. GORDON'S.

EDITORS BANNER OF LIGHT : The following is an account of a *séance* held at the rooms of Dr. H. C. Gordon, 406 Fourth avenue, which, as secretary for the circle, I have been authorized to send you, with a request that you publish the same in the *Banner* at your earliest convenience. I have the original signatures in my possession, and any person can see them by calling upon me at my address.   Respectfully yours,

EDWIN A. QUICK.

61 WEST 18TH STREET, NEW-YORK, }
  December 30, 1872. }

The undersigned, from an earnest desire to assist in spreading the truth, and from a sense of justice to a medium, very cordially bear testimony to the occurrence of the following *facts*, which we severally witnessed at the rooms of Dr. H. C. Gordon, 406 Fourth avenue, New-York, on the afternoon of December 29th, 1872. There were present, besides the medium, ten gentlemen and three ladies.

The first spirit-form appearing—whose hair and beard gave evidence of the snows of many winters, and who was clad in Episcopal robes—was said to be Bishop White, the controlling guide of the medium ; an Indian woman then appeared, and after advancing and receding twice, permitted Mrs. M. J. Beaudine to place her hand upon her [the spirit's] head, when it vanished almost instantly. During the afternoon, a female spirit-form was developed, who finally advanced, passing in front of three persons to within six inches, and directly in front of her father, Dr. F. E. Andrews, who distinctly recognized her as his daughter. This spirit remained visible for the space of seven minutes, thereby giving all present an opportunity to see her very plainly. After this effort, the medium sank to the floor, apparently very much exhausted. These were not simply *flat* pictures, but the head and shoulders (and in some instances, part of the body) were *fully developed.*

In conclusion, we wish to say that every opportunity was given us to examine the rooms and surroundings, and we make this emphatic declaration : *We know that we were not imposed upon nor deceived.*

WILLIAM H. WHEAT,	JAMES H. MONCKTON,
CHARLES WINTERBURN, M.D.,	HENRY BUDLONG,
MRS. ANNA RICHMAN,	J. H. SHEILDS,
JAMES BURSEN, M.D.,	HENRY WHITHALL,
WILLIAM MILLS,	MRS. M. J. BEAUDINE,
EDWIN A. QUICK,	MRS. N. D. MONCKTON.

Who could doubt ?

"The Committee" was represented here but once. Untoward events prevented a repetition. They realized the sensation of a cat in a strange garret. Also that

> " Decorations of the golden grain
> Are set to allure the aged fowl in vain."

At the opened folding-doors, nearest the manifestations, was a table, at which sat a circle of believers, including several ladies, placed to the right and left of a vacant chair, to be occupied by the medium when desirous of obtaining more "magnetism." This is the subtle fluid through which the spirits work. It will be seen that our desire is to instruct as well as entertain. These ladies reposed in a sublime faith ; they did not scrutinize closely. They also retained their seats, which made it embarrassing, since, to get near those "manifestations," it would be necessary to go over those ladies, faith and all. While the faithful were coming in, and contributing their dollar apiece, the medium was dressed in a blue gown, extending to his feet, with a university cap, likewise blue, and a waistcoat, from "Leo and Lotus," very pronounced. Until the dollars ceased to flow, he moved around within his temple, without any visible purpose, occasionally seating himself at the table and heaving a profound sigh, which was echoed in the bosom of a young lady of fifty, seated at his side. He finally wrote on a piece of paper, and handed it to a pale young gentleman, who proceeded to play a variety of popular airs on a melodeon. The ladies sang a variety of airs, not popular, while the circle joined hands and went through a variety of contortions. The medium then wrote again ; this time a salutation from Bishop White, who, it seems, had appeared on the surface, but had not yet struck the retina of any one present. The bishop was glad to see us, but as he had so much the advantage of us, his greeting was received in silence. The medium then arose, retired to his sanctum, and, turning down the lights therein, changed his gown and commenced some performance, which could not be seen, as only a dim outline of his form was visible. A tall gentleman, of inquiring mind, arose and turned down the gas in the room where we were seated, and as this made the light around the altar the stronger, the "conditions" were destroyed, and the "doctor" came out of his trance, and returned to the table in a normal state. The light was turned up again, and precautions were taken against a repetition of the outrage, which was calculated to bring the spirits into stronger relief than they were accustomed to, and the medium resumed his unconscious condition. Farther occult performances around the altar followed, not visible to the audience, which sat in solemn stillness, awaiting events. Soon he appeared behind the gauze, clad in a long white robe, not unlike a surplice, but of sufficient fullness to inclose two or three persons, of his own size. By his side, and, as near as could be seen in the dim light, clasped in his extended arm, which was covered with the folds of the gown, hovered a figure with the face of a young woman. It was devoid of expression, and with that stiffness of contour peculiar to masks or automatic figures, and yet an enthusiastic lady recognized it as the face of her daughter, and "wished to state" that it frequently appeared to her in the street, and at her home ; that the features were as familiar to her as when on earth. After the exhibition had continued for a few minutes, the medium retired, with his "spirit," to the darkness surrounding the altar. Other faces were shown, in the same manner, and afterward, upon the long kneeling-board of the altar, was seen the form of a "spirit-bride," extended at full length, and in bridal-robes. The picture was touching, and excited much admiration.

While this was going on, the ladies were singing, mostly in falsetto, "Angels now are hovering round," "A charge to keep I have," and other orthodox hymns. The exhibition over, the gas was turned up and the medium appeared with a censer in his hand, and, lighting the incense, waved it in front of the altar and above the floor where he had stood with his spirits ; at one time stamping with the ball of his foot as though scrunching a cockroach. This over, he seated himself at the table and wrote a communication from Bishop White, promising a different order of manifestations, more wonderful and convincing than ever before. He then came out of the trance and the *séance* ended.

Though this man's recent exposure has been thoroughly ventilated through the press, I have given the details of the exhibition to show upon what puerile mummeries, palpable frauds and absurdities, many of the Spiritualists build their faith. To the eye of common sense, these figures, exhibited with all the surroundings necessary to deceive the vision, were as easily explainable as any series of tableaux, arranged in a parlor for an evening's entertainment. There was not a single wonderful thing about them, not even a sleight-of-hand trick, and yet hundreds of Spiritualists, including many who claim to be men of sense, were deceived by them and fancied they really saw spirits of the departed.

"The Committee" determined to go once more and then to see if those "spirits" were not as tangible to feeling as to sight. All the necessary arrangements were made, but happily we were forestalled. A party of gentlemen—all Spiritualists and yet not to be gulled by such palpable humbugs—sprang in upon Gordon at the opportune moment and obtained possession of the "spirit" then in hand, and, searching through the apartments, found all the paraphernalia, including the masks and figures he had used. These were subsequently exhibited at a conference of Spiritualists at Apollo Hall, in this city, and though there were, even then, found some who were ready to excuse and justify him, it was generally admitted that he had practiced deception. The majority, however, seemed to entertain the opinion still, that he was a medium of rare power, but had been influenced by evil spirits.

R. W. FLINT.

It has, no doubt, ere this been observed that the various media have their specialties, and that the spirits, probably with a view of promoting harmony, do not trespass upon the domains of each other. As with the necromancers, they all have their peculiar "manifestations," and, though in process of continued "development" for years, and receiving communications from every class of spirit, and, very often, from the same spirits, no medium ever performs as his neighbor does. In other words, each continues his little round of tricks, year after year, and, finding they answer his purpose, makes no change in them.

Another class of media, whose pretenses, in the mind of common sense people are shattered by the simple statement of them, are those who answer "sealed letters." That is, those who answer communications contained within several inclosures, sealed with any number of seals and any amount of mucilage, and, as alleged, read by the agency of spirits without being opened.

Of this kind is Mr. R. W. Flint, who has an office on Broadway, and whose terms are two dollars and three stamps. The attention of "the Committee" being called to him, a package was prepared containing the same question addressed by a son to his father, which Mansfield had pretended to answer. It was placed within five envelopes, several of which were tied around with a string, and sealed with a great number and variety of seals, and taken to him. It was retained in his possession for a week. When asked why this long time was necessary, he responded that the communications must be answered in turn, and showed the inquirer a large number he had on hand, inclosed in a great variety of ways—some in iron, others in tin and closely riveted. "Do you answer these?" was asked. "Certainly," he answered. From the fact that at different visits made by the members of "the Committee" at intervals of longer and shorter duration, the same packages were shown, a conclusion was pardonably drawn that they were made up for the occasion. At the end of a week, the question was returned with an answer showing a knowledge of it, but furnishing no information save that, contrary to what Mansfield had said, it stated two persons were engaged in the murder. Farther than this, it was but another form of "spirit of father present ; happy to communicate with his son ; can not answer question without investigation ; control of medium not good ; happy to see son interested in great truths of Spiritualism ; will communicate more freely next time." The seals, strings, and mucilage, however, seemed all intact. This puzzled the Committee for a time and until the experiment of opening a similar one was tried. It will hardly be thought necessary to go into a detailed account of the results of the experiment and the means used to open letters and restore them to their condition as originally closed. Dishonest post-office employees and others have done this with success for many years. Suffice it to say, that sealing-wax, made intensely cold, will easily separate from the paper on which it has been used ; mucilage and glue can be softened by the application of steam ; and a little ingenuity and a careful observation of the exact condition of the inclosures, when received, makes the operation an easy one. In the opening of letters, as hereinafter described by the "medium" of the Committee, no other utensils than such as are found in an ordinary business office, and the steam from the heater, were used.

A question, inclosed in several thicknesses of tissue paper and stitched down with a sewing-machine, made "the conditions" so bad that Mr. Flint could not get any "magnetism," though he tried, and it was not answered.

"DR." PARKER.

Hearing that the spirits had learned to control the telegraph and communicate through it by means of a young medium at the house of Dr. Parker, on Forty-sixth street, and thinking it of interest as tending to the advancement of science, "the Committee" proceeded thither in a body with precipitance. Ushered into a parlor, we were greeted by the doctor, an old gentleman of shabby exterior, who professes to cure all diseases by clairvoyance and mediumistic power. On announcing the object of our visit, we were shown into an adjoining room, and a circle was formed. A number of Spiritualists were present, among them a seedy gentleman who had been a Methodist preacher, a doctor, lawyer, farmer, judge, and a variety of other things. A wire from a battery in a closet and connecting with an instrument was carried around the circle and grasped in the hands of every person. In this manner we sat for half an hour, but the anxiously expected ticking by spirit-hands was not heard. The medium then began to tap on the table, in pretended use of the telegraph alphabet. Unfortunately for this small effort at deception, one of the gentlemen present was a practical operator, and, of course, at once detected the fraud. He then announced that "the conditions" were bad, and no manifestations of this character could be had. Upon being applied to, the spirits agreed to move the table, and another long sitting followed without result, until, at their request, the room was made perfectly dark. After an interval, the table began to tip, and the member of "the Committee" sitting near the medium perceived that he was tipping it. Attention was suddenly called to the beautiful stars shining in one corner of the room. All looked in that direction, and, true enough, there were two stars plainly visible to all, shining with a certain flickering light very peculiar. "Don't break the circle!" exclaimed one of "the Committee," who was seated between two of his friends, at the same time dropping quietly on his knees to the floor and beginning to creep around to discover the cause of those stars. This was soon accomplished, and taking a pin, he inserted it into a minute hole in the panel of a side door, and the stars went out suddenly. The light burning through this small hole, only perceptible when the eye was on a line with it, struck on a mirror or some other reflecting body, and was thrown upon the wall in the locality mentioned. Meanwhile, as no manifestation could be had from the spirits, it was concluded to render them some assistance, and thenceforward the table tipped, at one time turning entirely over ; raps were heard in every part of the room ; the ex-preacher distinctly felt the grasp of a spirit-hand on his shoulder and leg, which he wished "to state for the benefit of those present ;" and all this without the slightest suspicion on the part of the Spiritualists present that they were the tricks of the unbelieving visitors. This sitting was subsequently referred to at a special meeting of believers as one of the most satisfactory and convincing that had been experienced by those present.

Many other media were visited whose pretensions had not even a transparent trick to support them : "Developing media," who pretended to bring out the inherent mediumistic tendencies of applicants in such manner as they desire, as writing, talking, singing, or materializing media ; clairvoyant and magnetic physicians ; lazy, ignorant women, starving on their pretense in tenement-houses, holding up impositions so transparent as to be painful ; men who, with little knowledge of the healing art, claim to be influenced by a familiar spirit in the shape of a big Indian, and give advice in a certain broken English, the like of which no Indian either living or dead ever used.

DR. FOSTER.

It has been a source of great regret to "the Committee," that the absence of the famous test-medium, Dr. Foster, has prevented their attending upon his *séances* and witnessing his manifestations. They are, however, consoled by the fact that the " doctor" has inadvertently lighted upon the spirit of investigation in his peregrinations, and has been, as is claimed, thoroughly exposed by Dr. Thomas Nicholson and Dr. J. R. Graves, of New-Orleans. For the benefit of those who have not visited him, we state that he too has his little round of tricks, of which " the blood-red writing on the arm," hereinafter referred to and explained, is one of the most prominent. The *exposé* mentioned takes up eight columns of a newspaper, and, of course, is too long for us to give any thing more than a condensed report of it, which we do by reproducing the following, which originally appeared in the New-Orleans *Picayune.* After some preliminary remarks on the subject of Spiritualism and previous *exposés* of pretended media, Doctor Nicholson says,

" I shall now proceed to give a description of my *séance* with the celebrated test-medium.

" I went to the St. Charles Hotel expecting to meet Dr. Rollo Knapp and others, to have a sitting with Mr. Foster. I misunderstood the time of our meeting, and as I was about to leave, I happened to see a well-known lawyer in the rotunda of the hotel, to whom I mentioned my purpose. I did not know that he was an intimate friend of Foster, and a real believer in the creed oi Spiritualism, which during the *séance* I found him to be. He wished me to make some convincing tests, which I decided to do, with a determination to use and deceive, if possible, the famous medium.

" He then wrote the names of three persons on three separate cards at the clerk's desk of the hotel, one of which he showed me. The cards were sealed in three hotel envelopes, which he handed me to put in my pocket, and we started to Mr. Foster's room, No. 83. I requested my companion not to mention my name, but to introduce me as Dr. ******, a friend.

"Mr. Foster required me to sit in a chair, close up to the table, and my companion sat opposite to him, saying he had proposed some tests which he had given me. I thought this a little hasty on his part, but thinking that the tests would be a fair illustration, I put them on the table. Mr. Foster seesawed them one after the other, in a conjuring sort of manner, across his forehead, and throwing one to me, he said, 'That is Mrs. Nelson, who died in Tennessee. Open it and see.' I found it to be true. This was the card shown to me before entering the room. Throwing another one to me, he said, 'That is Mrs. Stephenson. Open it and see.' It was true. 'And that is W. P. N. Open it and see.' This was true. 'He is standing by you,' said Mr. Foster. Now I thought my time had come for a genuine test. I told him I would write him the name of a dead friend, to see if I could get a communication from him. Instead of doing this, however, I wrote a note to my companion, stating that I intended to test whether P. N. was really there or not. I said in the note that I did not know Mr. N. intimately, but would say that I was very intimate with him to Mr. Foster, and that I had done such services and acts of kindness to him that he would give some token of gratitude and tell Mr. Foster my true name. I carefully folded the note and gave it to my companion to put in his pocket. I did this because I did not intend that Mr. Foster should say that I would not acknowledge the 'facts.' I then wrote five fictitious names, one of which was Dr. Wadsworth, the only one with Dr. prefixed to it. I admit that Mr. Foster requested me to write my own name, which I did not ; for I decided to follow the advice of the celebrated philosopher Descartes—namely, in the investigation of the unknown, never to accept any thing as true which we do not clearly know to be so. That is to say, carefully avoid haste or prejudice and to comprise nothing more in our judgments than what presents itself so clearly and distinctly to the mind that we can not have any room to doubt it.

"Handing the names openly to Mr. Foster, I remarked that if Mr. P—— N—— was present, he would select my name, for he was intimately acquainted with me, and the services and kindnesses which I had rendered him were of such a character that he would certainly manifest some gratitude. Mr. Foster tore the names off the slip of paper separately and rolled them between his thumb and finger into pellets, threw them upon the table, and picked up this one and that one, saying, finally, 'Is this it? Be sure. You say this is it?' He threw it to me, at the same time going off into a mediumistic swoon, spasmodically grasping my hand, exclaiming, with intense emotion, 'P—— says he will never forget your services and kindness to him, and he will follow you spiritually to the grave to bless you.' (!!!) Now, Dr. Wadsworth was not my name, nor had I ever benefited the lamented gentleman whose spirit Foster pretended to be present and speaking through him.

"How could I have deceived the spirit of P—— N—— and Mr. Foster too? And why would Mr. N——make such a huge fool of the world-famed spirit-seer? 'The fraudulent imposture foul' is too glaring. This one 'fact' alone is such a powerful negative against the claims of Spiritualism as to annihilate its pretensions to truth.

"When I informed him of the deception, his face was blood-red, and he became very angry. After my companion quieted him, he was willing to let me proceed further. But he tried to make it an absolute condition that I should ask questions that were genuine. I consented vaguely, and with a bucketful of mental reservation.

"Again I assumed to be writing names, but I wrote another note to my companion, saying that I wanted to see if the spirit of Mr. Alford was present, a fictitious person I knew no more about than I do the gentleman in the moon. Handing the note to my companion, I folded up the name of Alford and gave it to Mr. Foster, stating if that gentleman were present, I would surely get a communication from him which would test the whole of these curious things. Well, I got a splendid manifestation from my dear departed friend, Mr. Alford ! Mr. Foster told me a great deal of Mr. Alford's regards for me. I endeavored to get a description of my spiritual-found friend, but alas ! Foster turned his attention to something else.

"I was afraid to say any thing about this deception. If I had, my *séance* would have ended. I 'made out,' as the children say, 'that it was all so,' and Mr. Foster, I was exceedingly glad to see, thought he had gained a glorious triumph. I wrote another note to my companion, saying I was going to try to get a manifestation from Mr. Henley, a being as fictitious as the ubiquitous Alford of spiritual fame. My companion put it into his pocket. Giving the name of Henley, which was folded up several times, I soon heard from this apocryphal spirit. Foster told me he was standing by my side, and he says 'his name is Henley.' (!) 'Mr. Foster, will Mr. Henley select my true name if I write it among several others ?' 'He says he will,' said Foster. 'Very well, sir; I will write them.' A few fictitious names were written, among which was my own. Mr. Foster treated them as he did the others, and selected Dr. Thomas Nicholson ! The inner temple of my being had generated so much humor that it was ready to burst. I could hardly proceed any further. The ridiculousness of the thing was getting too Quixotic. I managed, however, to get to my father, about whom I felt the awe of natural impulse.

"I prepared another note for my companion, telling him my father's name was George Nicholson, and if he were dead at all, I had good reason to believe he had died in Liverpool, England.

"I asked Mr. Foster if my father were present. 'Your father is standing by your side.' 'Well, where did my father die, Mr. Foster?' He gave me no answer, but told me to write the name of the place he died at among others, and ne would select the time and place. I wrote several places in America, and Manchester, England. He selected Manchester. I told him no. 'Did you put the real name of the place he died?' 'No sir.' That worked him up to another rage. He demanded that I should write the right place. I pledged him that I would. He finally selected Liverpool, but had selected Mobile and Dublin before. I told him that it was impossible that my father could have died at the four places pointed out by him. He tried to throw the fault on me for deceiving. As a desperate finality, I said I did not know whether my father was dead or alive. This ended the scene. He got up from the table and paced up and down the room very angry. He would not, by any persuasion, accept my $5! There are several gentlemen of the city, whom I can mention, who have detected this self-asserting test spiritual medium.

"I had unconsciously made a complete catspaw of my companion, but Foster would not listen to the notes in his pocket.

"Dr. J. R. Graves devotes eight columns of his paper in exposing the impositions of Foster. I will only quote the following at present. Dr. Graves says,

" 'After some time, he again looked toward me and said, "George Snyder, have you no relative by that name!" "Yes, sir; what does he wish?" "To speak to you." "Is his name Dr. George Snyder?" "Yes, sir; that's his name—

Dr. George Snyder." " Will he tell me where he died ?" A long silence; but Mr. Foster busily engaged answering others. Finally, "Mr. Foster, you keep the doctor waiting a long time ; he is an impatient spirit unless greatly changed since last I saw him. Permit him to answer my question." "He says you must write down several places, and the correct one among them, and he will indicate it." I did so, and folded the slips and handed them to Mr. Foster, who soon returned "Memphis." I called the special attention of the gentleman sitting by my side to the answer, when Mr. Foster anxiously asked me if it was correct. I informed him that Dr. George Snyder had dined with me an hour since, and if this was indeed his spirit, he had died within the last hour. The company was only momentarily stunned, but each eagerly urged him to obtain answers to their questions.'

"Mr. Foster had no more communications for me during the rest of the sitting !"

THE COMMITTEE'S MEDIUM.

"—Ways that are dark
And for tricks that are vain."

I have stated that, as the various tricks of the media were discovered, one of the members of " the Committee" began to practice them—the object being to show how easily they could be performed and people be deceived thereby. We had observed that every medium had a familiar, in the spirit of a departed wife, or brother, or early love, which acted as a messenger in hunting up absent spirits, gave response to questions in the pretended absence of those called for, generally finding fault with "the conditions," and advising the visitor to come again. In a word, this familiar is used to tickle the fancy of people, induce them to return by promises of some wonderful manifestation, put them off for a time, and so avoid inconvenient questions, and give time for investigation into the habits and associations of the sitter, if it should be thought worth while, in order to astonish him on some future occasion. As a test of this, many experiments were made, which, we well knew, would nonplus the medium, and never in a single instance did "the familiar" fail to come to the rescue, generally stating, through the medium (of course) that "he is exhausted ; the spirits will not control to-day ; the conditions are bad ; come again," and so on, *ad infinitum* and *ad nauseam*. Our medium therefore found it necessary to have a familiar, and so selected "Kate Hughes," that being, in his estimation, a euphonious and pretty name, and thence-forward "Kate" was kept very busy in performing the duties of her class as described. No admission of trickery was at first made ; all the manifestations were received by "the Committee" with entire gravity and commented on as wonderful. The fact that a new medium had appeared, with wonderfully versatile powers ; indeed, not—as were the others—confined to any specialty ; a gentleman of wealth and social position, who made no charge and was therefore beyond suspicion, was whispered around among "the faithful ;" and as Spiritualists are never satisfied, but always seeking new tests, applications from them for a sitting were many and persistent. There was just enough difficulty placed in their way to stimulate curiosity, but the applications were always granted in the end, and not once was the fact of his being as wonderful a medium as reported questioned. The calm, steadfast, rapt expression of his face, growing gradually paler in his awful communion, was noticed and commented upon. Around his head was seen a halo of light from which looked out spirits of seraphic loveliness. Placing his hand on a folded paper, containing a question, *à la* Mansfield, he adopted the style of that distinguished gentleman—only not lolling out his tongue, as having an unpleasant effect—and wrote answers to hundreds of questions, giving messages from long departed and forgotten friends, concerning whom the visitor was ready to swear the medium could not, by any possibility, know any thing. Raps were heard about the room, the furniture moved, ghostly vapors made the air thick and redolent of spirit presence. Slates were obtained, upon which "spirits" wrote, under the table and on top of it, after the closest examination by the sitter, and without its being "out of his sight" for a moment. A clear explanation of how this could be accomplished was one moment given a visitor, and to his entire satisfaction, and the next, he would be bewildered and mystified by something inconsistent with such explanation, and more startling than he had seen before. Amid it all, "Kate Hughes" was as active as a "little busy bee," now running off into space in search of somebody's grandmother, again settling some point of spiritual philosophy ; defining the status of Jesus and Mohammed ; rebuking a doubter ; explaining an inconsistency, and promising better "manifestations" on another occasion. She could control the medium when no other spirit could, and a nice though very busy time she had of it.

Late one afternoon, after a variety of "manifestations," in the presence of many persons, and while they were being thoughtfully discussed, a knock was heard at the door, which, being opened, admitted a stranger of most respectable appearance. He seemed somewhat astonished at the company present, but at once introduced himself, and was recognized by his name as a gentleman of great prominence in the financial world. After a short preliminary conversation, he stated that he had been informed of a spirit-medium there, who answered questions in sealed inclosures, and he had called to submit one. He was told that such things had been done, and was requested to write his question. "No!" he said, "I have it all prepared," and drew from his pocket an inclosure, made of blocked-tin, and securely soldered down. At sight of it, many of the Spiritualists, who were in entire sympathy with the medium, began to protest and talk about "conditions," etc. Such members of the Committee as were present remained calm, having an abiding faith. The medium took it in his hand, and stated that no such test had been submitted to him, and he could not tell. He held it for some time, placed it upon the table, covered by his hand, and gazing at the ceiling with a far-off, dreamy look, exclaimed, "We can answer it, but it will be necessary to form a circle." This was done, some twelve or fourteen sitting around and holding one and another's hand. The medium retained the inclosure in his grasp, and after a few moments became very much agitated and convulsed, and, turning to the table, wrote a detailed answer, involving the recital of a number of circumstances, and the mention of dates and names. After letting the pencil fall, and glancing over the communication, he re- marked to the gentleman who had brought it, "This is not addressed to you, sir." "No?" said the other. "Well! I didn't know but there might be something in this idea of 'thought-reading,' and I requested a friend to write it. I do not know what it is." Naturally, much anxiety was felt to see the question. After much difficulty, the inclosure was opened, and the question was found to be addressed to the name that was signed to the answer, and each pertinent to the other. The gentleman who had written the question subsequently stated that he had never written or spoken of it to the medium or any one else, and that the answer was entirely correct. Naturally, the Spiritualists were much delighted, and, as usual, convinced. On another occasion, a question, inclosed in a bar of soap, was answered with equal facility. A gentleman of experimental tendencies, having some vague theory about electricity and non-conductors, submitted a question inclosed in a glass vial, imbedded in a block of wood, and thoroughly sealed. A number of Spiritualists were especially invited in to witness the experiment. A circle was again formed and an answer written, which gave a detailed account of the death of a gentleman by a railroad accident; how his body was so charred by fire as to be unrecognizable, and that it was only identified by his watch; his place of burial was also mentioned. This was found to be correct in every particular. Two of these inclosures were taken to a conference at Apollo Hall and publicly exhibited, as convincing evidence of spirit intercourse.

The success of this "medium" in answering sealed communications sent in by various parties was equally great. A large number and variety of seals, etc., were used, but afforded little difficulty in opening them. Several "tests" were offered, consisting of questions so inclosed that the writers were confident they could not be opened without detection. Of this class was one sent in by Mr. P——, a well-known Spiritualist of this city. He had inclosed it within a number of envelopes, the last being very ingeniously sealed with brass eyelets, perforating the paper containing the question on the two sides of a small envelope. These eyelets also inclosed on either side a circular piece of blotting-paper, tightly glued to the envelope, and very likely to be injured from the slightest tampering. Extending around the envelope and securely pasted were thin slips of paper of a peculiar character, manufactured especially for the use of the questioner in his business, very easily torn, and, of course, almost impossible to replace. He admitted that he had furnished no spiritual medium with any such test. Notwithstanding the difficul-

ties, it was opened, the question read and replaced. It was
subsequently returned to Mr. P——, with the usual response of the media when they fail, "I get nothing." He
smiled a significant smile, and, opening the outer inclosures,
was satisfied it had not been tampered with. He was afterward furnished with an answer which astonished him.

The well-known and belief-exciting manifestation of
"blood-red letters on the arm," referred to in the description of Foster's performances, had an amusing illustration
on one occasion. Our "medium" was in a private parlor,
where were gathered a party of ladies and gentlemen, who
were shown a variety of manifestations. Among them was
an unbeliever of emphatic manners, whose only reply to
demands on him for an explanation of certain marvelous
things was, " 'Tis all stuff and nonsense !" He was urged
to write a question himself, which he for some time refused
to do, but in the end assented. The "medium" took it in
his hand, raised his eyes to the ceiling, and assumed the
rapt expression for a moment, placed the paper to his
forehead, gave a convulsive shiver, and exclaimed, in a
sepulchral tone, "Would you know to whom your communication is addressed? Bare my left arm !" This was
hurriedly done, and there, in plain red letters, stood out a
name. "Would you hear the answer?" he continued, and
then proceeded to recount certain circumstances at some
length, which afterward proved a complete and truthful
answer to the question. "That happened before the medium was born," said an elderly lady present conversant
with the facts. The questioner was "dumbfounded," and
every body else convinced. This trick is performed in one
manner by writing with a pointed instrument upon the
arm, and afterward rubbing it briskly, which brings the
blood to the surface, and causes the letters to appear.

There are, however, other and better means of accomplishing it.

"Touches by spirit-hands" is another manifestation which the "medium" early acquired. His method, which is the same as that used by the impostors, is to form a "dark circle," the sitters being close together—knee to knee. Any number may sit, but four or five is better for the purpose. Each then places a hand on the shoulder of his neighbor, to the right and left, so that every hand may be engaged, and no collusion possible. This, with the exception of the medium, upon whose head is placed the palm of the hand of the one sitting next to him on the right. The arm of this one, so extended to the head of the medium, is then tightly clasped by both his hands, the one partially covering the other, and the under thumb raised so as not to touch the arm. Clasping tightly for a few moments, the circulation is impeded, and the arm becomes slightly numb. The medium then gently lets fall his under thumb upon the arm, and, at the same moment, raises his upper hand, which is then at liberty, while the owner of the arm realizes no change in his sensations, but believes and will readily testify that his arm was clasped by both hands every moment. The "medium" can now use his disengaged hand as he chooses, taking care not to relax his grasp with the other. He can lightly touch the shoulders or heads of those near him, finger the strings of an instrument, throw something across the room, and, with the aid of the imagination of his company, apt to be abnormally excited in the dark, do all the wonderful things concerning which we hear so much in connection with this "manifestation."

It would be tedious and useless to give in detail all the manifestations given by the medium. Suffice it to say, that no manifestation was shown us in our investigations which we did not repeat many times. And further than this, we produced as many samples of wonderful and unaccountable phenomena, showing knowledge of facts and names of which "the medium could know nothing," etc., as ever did any of the media in the same length of time.

In my description of certain of these "manifestations," I have spoken of them as they appeared to the uninitiated observers, not thinking it necessary to explain the "way and manner," as it certainly is not now to say to the reader that they were all the result of trick and collusion.

CONCLUDING OBSERVATIONS.

In closing this investigation, "the Committee" desire to call attention to a few well-ascertained facts, which, independently of our discoveries of trickery, at least tend to preclude the idea that the manifestations of the media are the result of supernatural agency.

And first, we wish to state that our experiences and their results are herein embodied for the benefit of those who are ready and willing to accept rational and natural explanations of phenomena. To the class—and it comprises not a few—which says to us, "Because you imitate the things which Mansfield and Slade do, it is no evidence that the phenomena in their presence are not the results of spirit agency, though they may be of trickery in yours," we have nothing to offer. We assume that, if we can show that all the pretended manifestations can be explained by natural causes, intelligent people will discard the idea of their being the work of spirits. Of others, we can only say, "They are joined to their idols," and we are willing to "let them alone."

We have found that the Spiritualists differ essentially as to who are genuine media, those upon whose revelations the faith is built. Some insist that certain ones are impostors, and others are fully convinced that the manifestations made through them are truthful and of spirit agency.

The clairvoyants who pretend to be under control of spirits, and to exercise a power of vision and perception beyond that of man in his normal condition, are as liable to be, and are, deceived as others, believing implicitly in the mediumistic powers of those afterward shown to be the most arrant knaves and cheats. An explanation of this is sought to be found in the statement that there are good and evil spirits which control the media, and this is called in to explain the myriad absurdities which are constantly appearing. It is not necessary to call attention to the fact that this entirely destroys confidence in any thing which "the spirits" may say, and that the faith built on the foundation of their revelations falls to the ground at once. There is, of course, no base for the statement; it is a pure assumption, and in this the Spiritualist is consistent. Among philosophers and men of science—whom these people despise, claiming to be "babes and sucklings," as contradistinguished from the wise—it is the custom to ascertain facts and then devise a theory in explanation, and in such proportion as it is consistent with the facts is it considered correct. But the Spiritualist, illogical in this as in every thing, invents both theory and facts.

Communications addressed through different media to the same spirit result in entirely different and inconsistent answers, and, though communications from one spirit are obtained through a dozen different media in succession, no one ever refers to any previous interview had elsewhere, but all start off with an expression of pleasure in being able to communicate, "have long desired to," etc., and this, though a long interview had taken place half an hour previously through another medium.

We have found that no statement of a believer in this monstrous delusion, touching any "manifestation," can be relied on, though he be ever so honest at heart. They invariably mistake the impressions they receive for facts, and, not infrequently, will claim for the medium what he never claimed for himself.

Noticing the intentness with which media are in the habit of listening to every word let fall, it became the custom of the members of " the Committee" to casually mention names, ostensibly of friends deceased. These were invariably reproduced by the respective media, on some other occasion, whether of real or fictitious persons.

The great successes of the media are constantly blazoned abroad, and the impression is created among the unthinking, that these are fair samples of their powers. The manifestations that are by no means remarkable make up the great mass ; but occasionally—for example—the medium somehow obtains a knowledge which enables him to surprise and startle. Names and circumstances are lugged in, not incidentally—the medium seldom having sense enough for that—but with a directness which betrays the purpose. And these are the tests which are made known to the world.

No medium has ever imparted any valuable information to the world. Our ignorance of the " Great Unknown" is as dense to-day as ever. It is claimed that media have given valuable advice to business men. Well ! This Committee can do that too. Farther, there have come to its knowledge several instances where immense sums of money have been lost by men who have been foolish enough to follow the advice of " spirits," given through media. It is, moreover, a sufficient answer to this pretense to say, what is well known, that these people, as a class, are among the most impecunious in society.

If any one will take the trouble to read the literature of Spiritualism or listen to a number of its orators, he will see that it has no well-defined doctrines, no creed ; that the theories and speculations are as various as those who entertain them are numerous, and, like the German metaphysician, its votaries evolve their ideas from the depths of their inner consciousness. Though, as they state, in constant communication with the beings of another world, few agree upon the character of that world, the condition of its inhabitants, or upon their aims and purposes. No Spiritualist is thoroughly satisfied of the truth of spirit intercourse with mortals. They are all "investigators," though they may have been professed Spiritualists for a quarter of a century. They are constantly seeking for new and more satisfactory "tests," and they resent any attack on their theories with a sensitiveness which evinces a consciousness of their weakness.

A theory very generally advanced is, that media are peculiarly susceptible to the influence of both good and evil spirits, and that they are not responsible for their actions when thus influenced. The grossest immorality is prevalent among some of them, which is sought to be excused by even certain upright and well-meaning people, on the ground that the spirit, and not the medium, is responsible. Numerous anecdotes, calculated to make the superficial laugh, and yet of the saddest moral, are told, showing the evil actions committed and the immoralities indulged in by both men and women under this pretended influence, and for which they insist they are not responsible. We need not point out how every prop of morality, every bulwark of society, is thrown down by this hideous assumption.

AN APPENDIX.

NATURALLY the *exposé* of fraud and charlatanism on the part of the most prominent media of the city or of the world, as it originally appeared, created a profound sensation among the Spiritualists, and the attendance at the regular weekly conference, at Apollo Hall, held on Sunday afternoon, the 16th of March, was very large. The usual platitudes were indulged in by a variety of speakers, who—probably out of regard for human life—are confined to ten minutes of time. Though they made no allusion to the *exposé*, it was evidently in the mind of every one, and an uneasy, agitated spirit was abroad. A young man finally arose, announced himself a "searcher after truth," and said he came there to speak about what appeared in that morning's *World.* This broke the ice, and a fearful onslaught was made upon "the Committee" by several speakers, the most virulent of whom were certain persons who had pronounced the "manifestations" through "our medium" the most convincing tests they had ever witnessed. We are pleased to be able to say that the more thoughtful and intelligent Spiritualists have been with us from the start, have manifested no disposition to uphold the cheats and tricksters we have undertaken to expose, but on the contrary, have sustained us in every way, and have furnished us with a great variety of valuable information, going to show the fraudulent character of the media.

Those who attacked us on the occasion referred to were especially emphatic in their indorsement of Slade, who had for them produced the manifestations of slate-writing many times without, as they alleged, ever touching the slate, and

they were ready to guarantee he would do it again. This
ied to the following correspondence :

LETTER TO DR. HENRY SLADE.

NEW-YORK, March 17, 1873.

DR. HENRY SLADE, 210 West Forty-third Street, City :

DEAR SIR: Yesterday, at Apollo Hall, we made the following proposition ; viz., that we would donate five hundred
dollars ($500) to any charitable institution which might be
selected by the members of the conference, on condition
that you would write or cause to be written a single line,
across a slate laid on top of a piece of pencil, placed where
we may desire to place it, upon your table ; the slate to be
furnished by ourselves, and your hands never to touch the
slate or the pencil. It is claimed by those who firmly believe it, that you have done this and more, and that you can
do it again. If you really can, we suppose you will be more
happy to be the means of contributing this amount to cha-
rity, than you would be to receive the ten dollars which
would otherwise be the cost of the *séance*, hence we expect
the *séance* free. It is, of course, expressly conditioned that
the writing shall be done in the presence of Mr. Grant and
Mr. Tifft, and as many others of our friends as you choose to
admit. We, however, insist only on the two. If you are willing to submit to this test, please inform us by bearer in
writing, naming any hour of any day this week (in the day-
time) when we can meet you, and we will call at your place.
Your kind attention and reply, giving us at least one day's
notice, so that we may arrange our business accordingly, will
greatly oblige, yours very respectfully,

(Signed)   J. N. TIFFT,

        WILLIAM G. GRANT, JR.,

        JOHN S. SCHULTZ, JR.,

        HENRY R. TIFFT,

        F. D. MERSERAU.

210 W. 43rd St. N. Y.
March 18. 1873.

Mr. J. N. Tifft and others.

Yours of yesterday containing your proposition made at Apollo Hall on Sunday the 16th inst. viz :

That you would donate five Hundred dollars to any charitable institution on condition that *I would write or cause to be written* a single line across a slate laid on top of a piece of pencil placed where you might desire to place it on my table—

The slate and pencil to be furnished by yourselves, and I am not to touch either slate or pencil.

In reply I must inform you that your proposition does not come within the province of any thing I might claim in regard to the manifestation of writing. that has repeatedly occured in my presence. Therefore I have no warrant or authority for accepting it—For obvious reasons. You propose that *I shall write* a line across a slate. or cause a pencil to write a line without myself touching either slate or pencil.

My dear Sirs you would have been just as consistent to have made this proposition to your nearest neighbor as you have been in making it to me—Because I claim the writing that has so often occured in my presence during a period of some years is a phenomenon over which I have no controll whatever.

Therefore I have no authority to say that it will occur again—

It is recorded in history and believed by many that on a certain occasion a hand appeared and wrote upon the wall.

Was either of the persons present charged with writing the ominous sentence ?

Or were they ever called upon to repeat it ? It is not uncomon for me to sit with persons for these manifestations and fail to obtain any

This is no disappointment to me—

But when they do take place my surprise can hardly be less than those who witness it for the first time—And were they never to occur again it would be no evidence against the genuineness of those witnessed by thousands of inteligent men and women whose testimony would be taken as evidence in any court of Justice upon any other question—

This it seems you are trying to overcome by declaring that you have failed to witness what others may have told you they have seen—

If that is satisfactory to you it certainly is to me. for I am fully aware that an acceptance or denial by one man or any number of men will make no difference with the facts.

It is unpleasant for me to attempt to discuss this or any other question, as it unfits me for the duties to which I am devoting my life—and the conditions you propose under the circumstances in this case would create that anxiety of mind with me that I could not for a moment expect the manifestation to occur.

I will say in conclusion your offer financialy considered is liberal.

And should you still be very desirous of bestowing it upon the needy, I trust you will have no difficulty in finding those to whome it would be acceptable.

Respt

Dr. H. SLADE *

Subsequently many of the intimate friends and ardent supporters of Dr. Slade endeavored to prevail upon him to

---

* This letter is reproduced here with all its excellencies and defects, as written. —AUTHOR.

attempt the manifestation. All were very positive he would consent. A number of "Angel Guides" informed their subjects that he would ; in substantiation of the great truth of spirit intercourse. But he didn't and wouldn't, and so the " great truth" suffers for want of this confirmation.

The Committee is willing the reader should draw his own conclusion from this correspondence, only desiring, in this connection, to say a word in reference to a manifestation which has been frequently called to our attention, and of which Dr. Slade speaks in his letter. We refer to the " Handwriting on the Wall." The Committee admit a certain degree of ignorance concerning it. It occurred some time since, and who the medium was is not stated. We have only to say : Had we been there, and been called upon to pay $5 for the exhibition, we should have made some inquiries. And here, too, we would call attention to the remarks of a Spiritualist, reported in the *World* of March 23d, as follows :

" Such a proposition as the one made to Dr. Slade is absurd, if there is any truth in the manifestations from spirit-land—a mere begging of the question. Just apply it to one of the miracles of old, and see. Moses went up forty days into the mountain, and was hid from the people in fire and smoke. When he returned, he brought the tables of stone, written on by the finger of God. Imagine a committee from the Hebrew laity, taking him by the beard and addressing him in the spirit of Slade, ' See here, Moses, that writing is very well done, but you were gone forty days in the mountain, and hidden all the time in clouds and sulphur smoke. Now we will put faith in the miracle, if you will let us furnish a couple of tables, and take a deputation from our number up into the mountain with you, do away with the clouds and smoke, and write, or cause to be written, a single law upon our tables.' The merits of the question of spirit-manifestations in fact, are precisely the same in one case as in the other, and the reply in each the same."

Though Spiritualists are energetic and persistent in their denunciation of the Bible, and stigmatize those who believe in it as a divine revelation, they are ever ready to go to it for facts, when it suits their purposes. Unlike them, we accept the venerable tradition referred to in the above extract, but we fail to see the parallel in the two cases. If Moses had been in the habit of going up into the mountain and bringing down stones with inscriptions, which he claimed were written by supernatural agency, and making the children of Israel pay $5 apiece for the exhibition thereof, we think a committee of the Hebrew laity would have been justified in taking a look inside of the cloud. This "Committee" certainly would have donned its "sandal-shoon and scallop-shell" at once.

We have, during the past month, received an immense number of letters, making inquiries, reciting tests, informing us of tricks on the part of certain media, discovered by the writers, and more than all abusing us, in a manner which savors more of the sensual and devilish than the spiritual and lovely. Although causing us much trouble and expense, we have endeavored to answer all such as have been addressed to us in the spirit of courtesy. To others we have paid no attention.

At this point we desire to state, that we entertain the usual opinion among gentlemen, regarding anonymous writers. Their communications find their way, at once, to the waste-paper basket, when addressed to us, without the compliment of reading.

We have thought a sample of the correspondence in which we have been engaged may be of interest here, and we insert one or two.

[From *N. Y. Herald*, March 30.]

THE EXPOSURES OF MEDIUMS.

TO THE EDITOR OF THE HERALD :

Is there no love of truth and fairness in the New-York press while treating of Spiritualism? The *Herald* has seemed most fair in giving all sides of questions, so I have appealed to it. If the papers must have sensations, why not attempt to slaughter some cause that is a little less sacred than the only one which pretends to give facts in proof of the soul's immortality? Lately the *Sun*, and still later the *World*, have attempted to expose our principal mediums, and show that they are all frauds, and although their correspondents have skillfully perverted facts to suit their prejudices, the *Times* has seemed to believe them and comes out editorially, signifying that mediums are impostors and Spiritualists a set of dupes who can not see into deception excepting when others show it to them. The stupidity of this insult may be seen when it is remembered that many of the most eminent men of science and letters of the day, many of the greatest geniuses of all ages, and all the monarchs of Europe admit the facts of Spiritualism, and entertain spiritual mediums. The seven "gold brokers" and others, who went out to get up a sensation for the *World*, by tearing down characters which are precious to thousands, say they have "friends and relatives," who, since they have become Spiritualists, have been "of little or no practical use to themselves or any body else," and that a desire to rid these people of a "delusion" exercised a controlling influence upon them. I do not wish to be personal, but it is not a good omen for them to have "friends and relatives" so inferior as to be injured by the beautiful facts of spirit communion, and, moreover, it would have looked better if they had possessed a supreme desire to ascertain the truth with

reference to these mediums, instead of having such a determination to put them down for the good of these friends.
But multitudes almost too great to number have received
benefits from Spiritualism—have been convinced of the
soul's immortality and glorious destiny—have been cured
of what were pronounced incurable diseases by all other
methods, and have had the fear of death completely dissi-
pated. The monarchs of Europe are also sufficiently advanced to see the benefits of Spiritualism; for the freeing
of the twenty million serfs of Russia, and the great movements for religious liberty in Austria and Italy, were
brought about through the hated mediums. But what have
these seven men of the world done? Have they loved truth
as did the eminent savant, Professor Hare, who proved this
matter through all kinds of machinery and experimentation
for years, through mediums, until he was converted from
his atheism? Have they equaled Judge Edmonds, who made
this great subject a special study of over two years before
he decided? Have they imitated the "Dialectical Society,"
which includes many of the greatest scientists of England,
and which, after forty meetings for investigation of the subject, decided that there was a power manifested apart from
all visible forces, and one which exhibited "intelligence"?
No; they are not that sort of men. They have manifested
great ignorance of the philosophy of mediumship to start
with, which they might have remedied if they had read
Mr. Hazard's treatise on the same. This is what they have
done:

First. They have perverted the truth with regard to Drs.
Slade, Mansfield, etc., by pretending to do all that they can
do, while they in reality counterfeit only the poorest part
of what hundreds of the sharpest and most intelligent men
in the country have seen these same mediums do. Thus, let
a stranger bring them a double slate of his own, place it on

an uncovered table in daylight, place a small pencil inside it, cause the small pencil to write by itself so that every stroke is heard, and then on opening it find a message written in English or French, and perhaps a name of a departed friend signed. This will be truly imitating one of Slade's difficult features. Further, I hold in my pocket a long slip of paper, on one end of which I wrote a question, and then after folding it ten times so that no mortal eye could read it, handed it to Dr. Mansfield, who answered it immediately, and gave several names of departed friends that no one in New-York, himself included, had heard of. Multitudes have had equal experiences, and fourteen languages have been written through his hand. But I have not space here to notice the slashing remarks about others, especially Foster, whom they admitted that they had not seen at all.

Second. These brokers and merchants, who, from their avocation, should understand the money market better than the subtle laws of mind, have after these brief investigations attempted to settle what scientists require years for, by blackening the characters of several much esteemed men, and have wounded the feelings of thousands who understand this subject far better than they. They are welcome to their reward. E. D. B.

THE RESPONSE OF "THE COMMITTEE."

[From the *Herald* of April 6th.]

THE EXPOSURE OF MEDIUMS.

To THE EDITOR OF THE HERALD :

As we are equally satisfied with your correspondent "E. D. B.," in his communication with the above heading, published in your issue of last Sunday, that the HERALD is fair in giving all sides of questions, we venture to appeal to it in response.

Though "E. D. B." sees fit to cloak himself under these

initials when attacking gentlemen whose names have been made public, yet it is easy to perceive from the tenor of his communication that he is a believer in the alleged manifestations, since, like the majority of that class, he deals in pure assumptions, without a single prop to support them, and in an entire perversion of facts. And first we challenge him to name one single scientist, recognized as such, who admits the assumptions of modern Spiritualism. It is true, some of them have admitted the fact of strange phenomena, but no one the explanation given. On the contrary, they have, with natural unanimity, especially disclaimed the idea of spirit agency. How men of science really regard this delusion may be gathered from the response of Professor Huxley to the Committee of the Dialectical Society of London, appointed to investigate and report on these phenomena, asking him to join it. He says, in effect, "In my investigations, which have been of considerable extent, I have discovered only gross ignorance or willful fraud, and, as far as I am individually concerned, I would rather live and be a crossing-sweeper than to become a spirit and talk nonsense through a medium at a guinea a *séance*." And Professor Tyndall, who recently went from among us, and whom we all so much admire, has expressed similar views.

As to the greatest geniuses of all ages, what their opinions may have been we will not stop to inquire, only, as Spiritualism celebrated its twenty-fifth anniversary last Sunday, if what "E. D. B." says is true, they must have believed in Spiritualism in the spirit of prophecy.

We confess our ignorance of the "beautiful facts of spirit communion," notwithstanding our many visits to the more prominent mediums with a view of learning of them. If they consist of table-tipping, writing nonsensical answers to foolish questions, playing a cheap accordeon with one hand under a table, then we have some knowledge; but after hearing many spiritualist orators, and reading much of the literature, we are ready to challenge its votaries to point out one new fact, new truth, or new thought which it has discovered or originated. There is not one. As has been said, "Its literature is a strange jumble of metaphysical jargon extracted from the limbo of worn-out creeds."

In reference to the report of the London Dialectical Society, "E. D. B.," as usual, tells only half the truth, and so leads the reader to an utterly false conclusion. While this committee admitted strange phenomena, so far from admitting the assumption of spirit agency, they called for further scientific examination to ascertain the true source, nature, and power of the force displayed, and its more prominent members—notably Mr. Edward W. Cox, in his *Spiritualism answered by Science*—have shown that the phenomena, including the "intelligence" manifested, were wholly inconsistent with the spirit theory.

We admit that Professor Hare was an eminent special scientist, and we state, moreover, that he is not recognized or quoted as an authority on scientific subjects ; that Judge Edmonds and Robert Dale Owen are men of intelligence. That so few of their class have accepted Spiritualism is an evidence that the age is breaking off the shackles of superstition. These men have proved as perfect a godsend to Spiritualists as has Fred Douglass to the colored race, and they are hurled at the head of disbelievers at every turn ; but, with feelings of high regard for these gentlemen, we respectfully decline to believe because they do, nor have we been able to find, either in their speeches or writings, any thing which convinces us.

It is no new thing for the monarchs of Europe to entertertain themselves with fools and jugglers. It has been the custom for some centuries ; happily in former times more than at present. That they continue to do so, may be cause for regret. It certainly can not be regarded as an evidence of the truth of Spiritualism.

As to the freeing of the 20,000,000 serfs of Russia and the great movements for religious liberty in Austria and Italy being "brought about by the hated mediums," we have only to say, in the language of the Scotch verdict, "not proven."

In reference to the investigations and exposures of mediums made by this "Committee," we would state that the manner in which they have been received by the more intelligent and thoughtful Spiritualists of Apollo Hall has been a sufficient reward. We do not claim to be men of science, nor was it necessary for the purpose of this investigation that we should be. We do claim to be able to detect fraud and expose trickery, and now repeat that every manifestation made by Slade, Mansfield, and others in the presence of the members of this Committee were mere tricks, which we have reproduced again and again in the presence of and to the entire satisfaction of more than a hundred of the intelligent Spiritualists referred to, as they will readily testify. And, further, we repeat that this committee have offered to Dr. Slade, and now offer to any medium, the sum of $500, to be devoted to any charitable object named by him or her, if he or they will write or cause to be written, or induce a spirit to write, one line or two words on either a single or double slate lying upon a table, in the presence of this "Committee," or any two members of it—the slate not to be touched by the medium after our final examination of it. And we further offer the same sum of $500, to be applied as stated, to any medium, if he or she will show or cause to be shown any manifestation or manifestations of any character whatever, which they ascribe to the agency of spirits, which this Committee can not explain and fully account for by natural causes, we being at liberty to pursue our investigation in our own manner. And herein, let us add, we feel quite as safe as does a certain gentleman who for a long time has had on deposit in Paris a large sum of money which he offers to any medium or clairvoyant who will describe it.

As to Mansfield and his fourteen languages, again "not proven ;" and if it were, it constitutes no evidence of spirit agency. A smattering of fourteen languages is not a wonder.   Very respectfully, yours,

J. N. TIFFT, 57 Broadway,
For the Committee.

A PRIVATE LETTER.[*]

MR. J. N. TIFFT, 57 Broadway, New-York:

DEAR SIR : I have noticed, from time to time, statements in the New York *World* in regard to a self-styled Committee, who have taken upon themselves to expose Mansfield, Dr. Slade, and other well-known mediums. You state in your letter in the *Herald* of yesterday, that you can do any thing that has been done through Mansfield. I would like to meet your Committee some evening this week, and test their powers.

I will give you below what was part of my first experience with Mansfield. August 21st, 1871, my wife passed from the mortal to the immortal. On the 9th of September following, I called at Mr. Mansfield's rooms on Sixth avenue. Mr. M. was an entire stranger to me, and I had no conversation with him save to receive instructions how I should write my question. I wrote on my first slip of paper, "Will my dear wife, Mary Ann Jones, communicate with me?" which I signed with my name in full. I folded this up several times, so that it would be impossible for Mr. Mansfield

---

[*] The names in body of letter and of writer are fictitious.

to read it ; as soon as he had pasted it up and placed his finger upon it, he began to write as follows, " Well ! my dear old friend J., I am with you, and recollect you kindly, and the many talks we had before I was so fully satisfied spirits of the departed could return and talk with mortals. Well ! I now have rid myself of all doubt. I do exist a conscious individuality. By and by I will tell you more. Charles has gone for Mary Ann—he will soon be here.—Z. W. THOMPSON."

The above was from one of my oldest and best friends, who was an inveterate skeptic in regard to a future life ; in fact, a Deist. He and I had spent many an hour investigating the phenomena of Spiritualism, and he was at the time of his death as confirmed a skeptic as ever in the past. I met him a few months before his death in Maine, and we had the same old argument over again. As I left him, I said, " Friend Thompson, the probabilities are that you will pass on to the unknown before I do, and if you do, I want you to come and tell me which of us is right and which is in the wrong." At this time I said to him, " I shall never ask for you ; you must come without calling." The communication is characteristic of him in every way. He was one of nature's noblemen—a gentleman of wealth and culture, and well read in the abstruse sciences. I had not thought of him, in any way, on that or previous days. The Charles that was mentioned was a mutual friend who had been dead fifteen years. I had no conversation with Mr. M. at this time, nor had he any means of knowing me or my antecedents. I went there for the sole purpose to see if my wife could talk with me through Mr. M., which she did to my full satisfaction. I had several other sittings with him, all of which were satisfactory to me. Now, I am neither a bigot or a fool. If you can produce, from the arcana of nature, any thing for me as straightforward and inde-

pendent as the foregoing, I should be very glad to meet
you and your Committee. I have not seen Mr. M. since I
had my visits with him. I believe in fair play, and if he is
a fraud, I would gladly aid in his exposure. Until so convinced, I shall believe him honest.   *   *   *

Yours truly,   JOHN JONES.

THE REPLY.

NEW-YORK, April 9th.

DEAR SIR : Yours of the 7th inst. is received and contents
noted. . . .

However correct you may be in other particulars, you
are evidently laboring under a delusion in supposing that
" the Committee" is at the beck of the public, or such portion of it as may desire to " test its powers." Notwithstanding
which, we profess ourselves ready and willing, at such time
as our engagements will permit, to meet any one who may
choose to call on us. We certainly do pronounce every
thing which Mansfield *did for us* the result of fraud and
trickery, and we are fully able to do the same things by
natural means. Farther than this, neither in the *Herald*
nor elsewhere, have we professed to go. Through an article
in the WORLD and at various meetings of the Spiritualists
at Apollo Hall, we have given the public the benefit of our
experience. It has cost nothing and the public is welcome
to it. We can not afford to deal with the experience of
others. We have therefore nothing to offer in explanation
of the " test" you refer to. The mention of names, you
speak of, in Mansfield's answer to your question, seems to
us but a repetition of a trick we have discovered to be very
prevalent among media, of ascertaining the names of departed friends of visitors, and then bringing them forward
at the opportune moment as an evidence of spirit agency.
We have practiced the same ourselves with success, and

have given strangers and believers what they declared to be the most convincing tests they had met with in many years of investigation. As we have been thus able to blind people, without money or price, and with a very limited experience, we are satisfied others can do it much better, under the incentive of one five-dollars secured, and many more likely to follow, and with the advantage of twenty years' practice in fraud. However, these suggestions are not offered to influence your mind, and if you are satisfied that Mr. Mansfield could have obtained a knowledge of the names mentioned, and the relations of the persons holding them to you, by none other than supernatural means, we can only envy you your facility for believing. Assuring you that we shall be happy to see you at the office of the undersigned, at any time between three and five o'clock P.M., I am very truly yours,

J. N. TIFFT,
For the Committee.

CPSIA information can be obtained at www.ICGtesting.com
Printed in the USA
BVOW02s1109171115

427457BV00001B/66/P